# Modern Streamers
# for Trophy Trout

# Modern Streamers for Trophy Trout

## New Techniques, Tactics, and Patterns

Bob Linsenman and Kelly Galloup

Foreword by Jerry Dennis
Illustrations by Richard Forrest

THE COUNTRYMAN PRESS
A division of W. W. Norton & Company
*Independent Publishers Since 1923*

For information about permission to reproduce selections from this book, write to Permissions, The Countryman Press, 500 Fifth Avenue, New York, NY 10110

For information about special discounts for bulk purchases, please contact W. W. Norton Special Sales at specialsales@wwnorton.com or 800-233-4830

Library of Congress Cataloging-in-Publication Data
Linsenman, Bob.
    Modern streamers for trophy trout : new techniques, tactics, and patterns / Bob Linsenman and Kelly Galloup ; foreword by Jerry Dennis. — 1st ed.
       p.   cm.
    Includes bibliographical references and index.
    ISBN 0-88150-466-1 (hardcover : alk. paper)
    1. Trout fishing. 2. Fly fishing. 3. Flies, Artificial.
    I. Galloup, Kelly, 1959–        . II. Title.
SH687.L5        1999
799.1'757—dc21
                                                              99–29642
                                                                  CIP

The text for this book was set in Adobe Garamond with Adobe Bernhard Modern for the display headings.

Cover design by Susan McClellan
Text design by Faith Hague
Illustrations copyright © 1999 by Richard Forrest
Jacket photos by Brian O'Keefe; inset on front cover by Bob Linsenman
Interior photos by the authors unless noted otherwise

The Countryman Press
www.countrymanpress.com

A division of W. W. Norton & Company, Inc.,
500 Fifth Avenue, New York, NY 10110
www.wwnorton.com

Printed in the United States of America

10 9 8 7 6

## Dedication

To my wife, Penny, who was extremely understanding of all the on-stream research that went into this book. And to my children, Madison, McKenzie, and Delaney Brook, who are too young to understand the draw of rivers, but hopefully will one day learn to love them as much as I do.

—Kelly

To Steve and Walt, two old pirates well past 40, who still fish hard and laugh like boys.

—Bob

# Contents

# Acknowledgments

M any people across the continent have contributed to the completion of this book. Their generous assistance with research, and thoughtful suggestions, criticisms, and validations greatly improved the end product.

Our deepest appreciation goes to Mike Craig, Jerry Dennis, Ray Schmidt, Steve Southard, Steve Pensinger, Doc Ellis, Rock Wilson, Greg Lilly, Jac Ford, Kelly Neuman, Scott Smith, Andy Busch, Penny Galloup, Dawn Kemp, Richard Forrest, and to Helen Whybrow, Jennifer Goneau, and the staff at The Countryman Press.

# Foreword

Jerry Dennis

For most of the first 30 or so years that I fished with a fly-rod, I was a pretty typical angler. I fished for trout, in rivers, with dry flies and nymphs, and I took special pleasure in casting to risers during hatches of mayflies and other insects. I kept a box of streamers in my vest, but I used them only when dries and emergers didn't work. If no bugs were on the water, I might clip back my leader, tie on a small Mickey Finn or a Muddler, and make a few casts. Like almost everyone, I cast down and across, let the fly swing, then retrieved it in short strips. I caught a lot of foot-long trout that way. Now and then I caught one as long as 16 or 17 inches. And once every couple of seasons I would hook a bigger one.

Then, a few years ago, I was invited to join a pair of remarkable anglers on a float trip down Michigan's Au Sable River. The Au Sable is the best-known trout stream in the Midwest, with a long history of quality dry-fly angling and a reputation for abundant hatches and oversized trout. In the 1950s, '60s, and '70s it probably supported more trophy brown trout than any river in the Great Lakes drainage. Unfortunately, it is not the river it once was. When you hear stories now about giant browns from the Au Sable, they're usually rumors.

But the two anglers I met that day in Mio, Michigan, weren't spreading rumors, and they weren't pining for the good old days. They talked about fishing the river now. They spoke of browns and rainbows over 20 and up to 30 inches in length. They told me about six-fish days—

six fish, that is, over 20 inches. They talked about the river as if it were still the trophy fishery of its heyday. They weren't bragging—you'll never hear Kelly Galloup or Bob Linsenman brag—they were just sharing the facts. And I believed them. I'd been hearing about these guys for years.

What really caught my attention that day on the Au Sable was the way they fished. They used streamers, but not like anyone had in my experience: They fished with them because they preferred to. They used 9-foot, fast-action rods and disc-drag reels loaded with sinking line. But most surprising to me was their terminal tackle. Their leaders were composed of a foot and a half of 20-pound-test Maxima for a butt section and 2 feet of 12-pound-test for a tippet. Their streamers were large and unfamiliar and seemed better suited for salt water than pristine trout streams. They cast them with pinpoint accuracy to the banks, splatting them a couple of inches from a log, or in the shadows beneath an overhanging cedar, or on the lip of a gravel bar. They retrieved the flies immediately, jerk-stripping them rapidly to the boat, then lifted the line, false-cast once, and banged them out again, precisely on target. They fished with intensity. It was physically and mentally demanding; I couldn't wait to try it.

But when mayflies began coming off and a few trout started rising, I picked up my dry-fly rod. Bob and Kelly continued throwing their big streamers while I made careful casts to risers and caught a few small rainbows. One or two went over 12 inches. I was ready to declare the day a success.

Then Bob hooked a 20-inch brown. It charged from a tangle of logs in a bend he and Kelly call Alligator Alley. We all saw it coming—broad and long as a fireplace log, flashing gold when it smashed Bob's cone-head Muddler and turned. We netted it quickly and released it.

Then Kelly hooked a 22-inch brown. It surged across slack, shallow water on the inside of a bend—water I had automatically written off as unproductive—and engulfed his Zoo Cougar in a swirl that stirred up the river for six feet in every direction.

I forgot about those dinky risers. I forgot about fine and far off, about delicate presentations. I began splatting giant streamers against the bank and yanking them through the water. Every cast I expected to have my arm jerked out of its socket. At Comins Flats a 15-inch brown smacked my streamer just as I was lifting it from the water. Not a trophy, but a nice trout. And it hit so hard that it threw water in my face. Adrenalin shot through my veins, making my heart pound and my hands shake. I've had the shakes ever since.

It's my good fortune that Galloup and Linsenman invited me along on a dozen or so outings while they worked on this book. On those trips I managed to catch more trout between 17 and 22 inches than I had caught in the previous decade. Once I even out-fished the boys themselves, taking a pair of 18-inch browns while they went fishless. What's more, a trout at least 2 feet long slammed my Woolly Sculpin a heartbeat after Kelly slapped the same pattern in the same spot without a strike. But that was an exceptional day. Other days it was Bob and Kelly who did the schooling. It'll be a long time before this student can expect to teach them anything—like the day hell freezes over.

Between them, Bob and Kelly have more than 80 years experience fly-fishing for trout, and it shows. They're among the most accomplished anglers I've met, but they're nevertheless in a class apart from other great fly-fishers. Most anglers will nail a few certainties about the sport, then cling to them. When we discover a tactic that works—even if it works only now and then, or even if it works just once—we pull it out and use it at every opportunity. Our inspirations become prejudices.

In contrast, the authors of *Modern Streamers for Trophy Trout* are anything but prejudiced. Their approach to fishing is consistently open-minded and creative. They accept nothing at face value. They're the most scientific anglers I know: once they identify a problem, they gather all the relevant data they can, formulate a hypothesis, and test, test, test. Much of their testing takes place on rivers and lakes—the best laboratories imaginable—but even when they're on land they're always experimenting at their vises, thinking, asking questions, imagining solutions.

As a result, they don't have much respect for the usual way of doing things.

Lucky for us, Linsenman and Galloup decided to collect some of their unconventional wisdom into a book. The result, which you hold in your hands, is the first fresh look at streamer fishing in half a century. As far as I know it's the first book ever to address effective ways to catch trophy trout, the toughest fish in fresh water. But it isn't a manifesto for slaughter. Implicit—hell, explicit—to the book's message is an appeal for conservation. I've met few people who love rivers and trout as deeply as Linsenman and Galloup.

And I've met few people who are as entertaining to fish with. These guys are more fun than the Swedish bikini team. When they fish, they fish, giving it their full attention and the full benefit of their experience and knowledge. But they don't take themselves too seriously, nor do they lose sight of where fishing fits into the Big Picture. Their banter is irreverent and relentless. No subject is sacred, no companion is exempt from gooning. If you get in a drift boat with this team, you'd better be prepared to laugh at yourself. And you'd better be prepared to see your preconceptions blown to bits.

*Modern Streamers for Trophy Trout* is a revolutionary book. It's fresh, fun, innovative, and probably a little dangerous. It might not make you give up dry flies and floating lines, but as sure as the day is long it will make your previously unproductive hours more productive. If you're like me, it'll give you a bad case of trout fever.

# Introduction

Bob Linsenman

There is a fly-angling paradigm, almost a cliché, that describes the process of a fly-angler's growth in terms of desires. First, we hope to catch *a* trout on a fly. Second, we want to catch *a lot* of trout on flies. Third, we want to catch *big* trout on flies. Finally, at the point of maturity, we revert back to the beginning—a trout on a fly. Certainly, any day that we catch a trout on a fly is a good day. But the paradigm suggests that we have lost our desire for big fish—which is not true. Every fly-angler wants to catch big trout. Lots of them, and the bigger the better. Catching a small or medium-sized trout is a very good thing, but catching a really big trout is a lot better. Don't you agree?

Of all the world's fly-rod glamour fish—steelhead, tarpon, salmon, bonefish, permit, muskie—trout are the most widely distributed and passionately sought. Big trout—trout over 20 inches—are dream fish. Whether fishing for cutts in the Snake, brookies in the Nipigon, rainbows in the Bighorn, or brown trout in the Housatonic, any and all fish of 20 inches or better make the heart beat faster and the camera click. A trout of 25 inches or beyond pushes the heartbeat like thunder; it makes the knees weak and the brain soft. Cameras overheat. Legends are born (it has been our experience that even the largest legend grows by at least 2 inches within 48 hours of release).

Trophy-sized trout generate such tremendous excitement simply because catching one is extremely rare, a true dream for 90-plus percent of fly-rod anglers. And the successful encounter with a trophy is a rare thing simply because the vast majority of anglers fish traditionally and predictably, casting to traditional "feeding lanes" and cover, which can be effective, but often is not.

Quite often, for reasons that we will explain in the following chapters, large trout are not where anglers expect them to be. Most fly-rodders fish dry flies—emergers, duns, or spinners—during hatch periods while the trophy browns and rainbows hunt smaller trout feeding on the surface. But it is this *stalking* trout, the trophy that slides in behind the unsuspecting 8-inch riser, that is the object of desire. It is an aggressive cannibal and not the least bit interested in a size 14 Hendrickson. Most anglers present their flies as food using traditional methods, such as the down-and-across swing, when big trout are not hungry but resting. What they need instead are specialized techniques to trigger an aggressive or defensive response.

Our own recognition of the wide variety of opportunities to take really large trout with streamers and subsequent development of specific tactics and techniques involved a degree of circumstance and luck, but the more important factors are continuing research and testing. We fish hard, every day we can get on the water. We have been avid fly-fishers for most of our lives, and for much of that period we have used streamers in the manner practiced by a high percentage of people—across and down, lazy swing, casual retrieve. We were killing time, waiting for the hatch and bored stiff.

Several years ago, upon my return from a busted steelhead trip to Ontario (torrential rain, floods, washed-out bridges), circumstance and luck collided to create my good fortune: Kelly Galloup, Jerry Dennis, and I were able to schedule a day's float on the Au Sable. It was late May. The water was slightly discolored, still quite cold but warming. I had previously fished for steelhead with Kelly and looked forward to this float for stream trout.

Jerry and I fished streamers and Woolly Buggers in the classical manner, the standard technique. We cast to traditional cover or to the deepest water and rather casually twitched the flies on a downstream swing. We caught a few small to average trout. Kelly, on the other hand, made at least two casts to every one of ours. He slapped the fly hard on the water, stripped fast, and jerked hard with his rod. He paused and jerked, paused and jerked. He cast to the bank, to the soft inside curves of sweeping bends, to the deep seams, to the shallows, to the featureless flow in the river's center. And long buttery copper forms swirled, charged, and slammed his fly. They came from everywhere and anywhere, some from expected lies like undercuts, but as many or more showed when least expected, from shallow tailouts, from flat, coverless runs.

When we stopped to rotate positions, Jerry and I looked closely at Kelly's fly. It was a yellowish sculpin pattern with an extremely wide head and a unique wing of dyed mallard flank feathers tied flat over the body. His line was a full-sinking class VI, and his leader was less than 4 feet long.

Although we each borrowed a fly from Kelly's box and mimicked his retrieve, we could not compensate for the line differential. Jerry and I both had sinking-tips and longer leaders. Big difference. Yes, we did better, moved more fish and bigger fish, but we did not keep pace with Kelly. We cast to the same spots with the same fly and at least a similar retrieve, but only Kelly's combination of full-sinker and short, stiff leader kept the fly at the proper level and carried the day. Clearly, Kelly had a complete system at work and our missing component affected our results. That day, the idea for this book was born.

The purpose of this book is to share what we believe are the key elements in the successful pursuit of trophy-sized trout. We will share with you the conclusions of our research on trout behavior, fly design, and technique. We will discuss why big trout behave differently, how they behave, and what impacts their behavior. We will examine why various fly designs perform different functions and appeal to a variety of trout triggers. Your understanding of the specialized techniques presented in this book will help you capitalize on the complex behavior of trout with fly and retrieve dynamics that heighten your chance of an aggressive response and a thrilling day on the water.

Some of our findings may surprise you (they surprised us) and seem at odds with conventional wisdom (such as it is), or at least with tradition. Others will likely confirm long-held suspicions. Big trout move differently, both in terms of distance and time, than most anglers realize; generally their behavior is a certain and radical departure from what the old-timers taught. Trophy-sized trout react to an intruder with much more aggression than you might imagine. And there are more *super* trout in most rivers than a dry-fly purist or dedicated nymph-fisher will see in a lifetime. But if you employ the techniques and tactics presented in this book, you will see them. You will notice a subtle shift in the bottom, a flash of dull copper and butter, perhaps crimson and pewter, a blurred, mouth-open charge. Your knees will shake.

～

We decided to write this book for several reasons. It fills a gap. There has been no new book on fishing streamers in decades, and there is very little information being published in the fly-fishing magazines. The volume of new information on large trout movement and behavior, on innovative pattern designs and fresh materials, and on radical techniques and tactics, needed consolidation for the benefit of fly-anglers. Although we are both professional guides and like to hold a few secrets, we feel an obligation to share. It is as much fun for us to observe a client's reaction to the charge of a big fish and its jarring take as it is to experience these personally—rod in hand. Both of us are *flies-only* anglers and guides who have been targeting trophy trout for many years. During the course of those years, each of us has been on the water, either guiding or fishing, approximately 200 days per year. With this book, we hope to share the excitement beyond our client base and to expand the joy.

Both of us have read the scientific reports and dissertations on trout movement and behavior. We have donned masks and fins in heavy current. We have experimented with pattern design and new materials. We have tried countless line and leader combinations. And we have studied the results of various retrieves under different conditions—changing the line speed, cast placement, and length of pause; using hand strips and rod pulses. We know what works and what doesn't. We have also consulted with expert anglers and guides across the continent. Ray Schmidt, Jerry Dennis, Kelly Neuman, and Mike Bachelder in the Midwest, Mike Craig and Greg Lilly in Montana, Steve Pensinger in Boston, and Tony Keltner in Maine are among the many who have helped with this project.

Our method of successful streamer fishing is an *active* hunt with specific tools and techniques. It is *not* the passive cast-and-swing method of days gone by, where you simply hope your fly might swing in front of a fish that might be hungry.

We have organized and written this book to be a practical guide. Each chapter presents key information that will help you in your pursuit of a trophy. An appreciation for the pioneers of streamer fishing, an understanding of large-trout motivation and behavior, and a knowledge of the impact of water and of hydraulic pressure on fish will give you a solid base of applicable knowledge. This, combined with our information on techniques, on new fly designs, and on specialized equipment will give you more success with the fabulous trout of your dreams.

A favor, please: Let them go. All of them. There is no justification for killing one of these magnificent creatures. Absolutely none. As alpha predators they are integral to every river's health; just the knowledge that they are present, like the wolves in Yellowstone, makes the fishing better.

Commemorate your success with images on film. Take careful measurements and a side-view, color photograph for a reproduction mount. Clip off the fly and stick it in your hat so you'll never lose it. Gently revive the monster. Stroke its flank as it glides away. Your fond memory of that fish will turn to boiling anticipation the next time you enter its territory. We promise.

# chapter one

# A Brief History of Streamers

Streamers are simply flies that mimic baitfish. Within the broad classification of *streamers,* the subclass *bucktails* are flies tied with hair and *streamers* are tied with feather wings. There is historical evidence that the first fly patterns were streamers, the most effective way to hook into large fish. Bone fragments and carved wood were relatively satisfactory for large lures in those days, but useless to the first angler who wanted to copy a blue-winged olive. The iron fishhook changed the game forever. Iron, then steel, provided variations of size and thickness that allowed artificial copies of smaller prey. The infatuation with insect patterns began.

The people who invented the first streamer flies caught fish to eat. If other game species were on the wane, it was catch fish or starve. We doubt that the earliest fly-anglers worried much about matching the hatch; they needed something fishy and meaty looking, something subsurface that would entice a respectable, lunch-sized victim.

The printed history of fly-fishing has largely concentrated on patterns and methods that deliver both terrestrial and aquatic insect imitations to feeding trout. Before Izaak Walton, there are a few interesting passages on angling by Aristotle, Rondelet, and others, but not much that would hold a contemporary angler's attention. It really all begins with Dame Juliana Berners who, according to Arnold Gingrich, the late founding editor of *Esquire* magazine and noted angling historian, "is to angling literature as Chaucer is to English literature, representing to all practical intents and purposes the very beginning." Her work, *The Treatyse of Fysshynge wyth an Angle,* first appeared about 1496. In terms of popularity with current angling historians, the next great work was Izaak Walton's *The Compleat Angler,* first published in 1653.

The very early writers set the tone for angling style and popular method that holds to this day. They described angling with 15- to 18-foot rods, and their favored techniques were aimed at allowing mayfly imitations to dangle and flutter across the surface. They created a popular sport with a prescribed order and plan of behavior that remains deeply ingrained.

*The Compleat Angler* popularized angling in England and Europe and, in fact, created the market for fishing books. On-stream innovation found its way into print. Robert Venables wrote *The Experienc'd Angler*—which, in 1662, was the first book to advocate the upstream cast. James Chetham followed with *The Angler's Vade Mecum* in 1681. He gave specific directions for night fishing and highly recommended examining a trout's stomach contents. Thomas Best's work, *Art of Angling,* first appeared in 1787 and enjoyed a run of 13 editions! Best suggested the use of a multiplier fly reel to quickly retrieve line. W. C. Stewart, another radical thinker, convinced the angling fraternity that upstream fly-fishing was the most effective approach; he also advocated rods of 10 feet, a full 3 feet shorter than the accepted norm of the day. William Scrope, in *Days and Nights of Salmon Fishing* (1843), wrote of the specialties required for urban angling (downstream London) and flavored his work with great anticipation and passion.

North American contributors to the early literature continued the introduction of fly-angling innovation. George Washington Bethune, who edited the first American edition of *The Compleat Angler* in 1847, recommended stealth and camouflage, and suggested a policy of stream ethics and courtesy. Thaddeus Norris's classic, *The American Angler's Book* (1864), was the first book to advocate catch and release—with instructions on how to do this so as to not harm the fish. Theodore Gordon is widely acknowledged as the father of truly American fly-fishing; although he fished with other methods, his real fame is centered on dry-fly fishing and his creation, the Quill Gordon. His streamer pattern, the Bumblepuppy, is an attractor by today's standards and is all but lost in the back of the closet.

Gordon leads us into the modern era—and little has changed. If you open the current issue of your favored fly-angling magazine—regional, national, international—you will find about 5,000 words on dry flies, wet flies, nymphs, and tying for every word on streamers.

The fact that the art of streamer fishing is often overlooked today in favor of more classical techniques may be a matter of conditional behavior prescribed by the patina of tradition laid down and polished by our ancestors from Walton to Uncle Jake, and by the perception of style as emphasized in today's journal texts and advertising. The notion that to fish "the hatch" is classy, contemplative, and cool is acceptable enough, and we enjoy it thoroughly; still, to ignore the excitement and reward of properly fished streamers is foolish. If you know how to work streamers effectively, and still prefer to exclusively fish bug patterns for smaller trout, that is your every right. But it is our intent to reach those who may want to fish streamers, catch bigger fish, and to experience a whole new world in fly-fishing.

Pioneers of streamer patterns and specific techniques have made significant and long-lasting, if not widely recognized, contributions to our sport. It is fair to say that the most important streamer pattern, in terms of overall, long-lasting impact, was conceptualized by Don Gapen while he sat on a rock on the shore of the Nipigon River in the late 1940s.

The Nipigon is a veritable factory for the production of large brook trout. Its flow runs (about) 12,000 cubic feet per second from its source at Lake Nipigon to its mouth at Lake Superior in western Ontario. The

Scott Smith

The Muddler Minnow is the classic example of innovative streamer design from the mid-20th century.

bottom is paved with sculpins, which provide the protein that brook trout need to grow quickly to significant sizes. Sculpins (family Cottidae) are bottom-dwelling, large-headed fish (also called bullheads) that frequent rock-bottomed streams. The large heads give them a distinctive body contour and profile. Gapen was an imaginative angler, and it is easy enough to envision his close examination of sculpins and subsequent experiments with materials and general shape. The clipped deer hair head that he eventually designed gave birth to an entire class of patterns loosely referred to as Muddler Minnows, the name of his original. No single fly pattern in all of fly-fishing has had a more significant impact.

From the Maritime provinces and New England, through New York, Pennsylvania, and the Great Lakes Basin, to the Rocky Mountains and on to the Pacific coastal waters, streamers have consistently produced the most significant numbers of trophy trout. Throughout the years anglers have conceived, tested, and refined their flies to meet regional requirements. Their applications of feathers, hair, silk, thread, and synthetics to the proper hooks now closely replicate the specific appearance and habits of baitfish.

⁓

This is not meant to be an inclusive history of streamers. We will discuss some of the major contributors while apologizing for leaving out everyone else. Our emphasis in this book is today and tomorrow. For a more complete history of streamers, we refer you to *Streamers and Bucktails* by Joseph D. Bates Jr., and for those interested in the pure history of angling, we have included several works in a suggested reading list at the back of this book.

You may recognize some of the following people as names attached to, or associated with, a particular pattern. Others are linked to other aspects of the sport; still others are "generalists"—writers, retailers, trout strategists.

Carrie Stevens originated the Gray Ghost to imitate the prolific smelt of Maine. It was an instant success and remains today one of the most popular fly patterns of all time. This is so not because the fly is beautiful (though it is!), but simply because it works. It has the proper wet shape and blend of colors, and trout love it.

No general attractor pattern is more justifiably famous than the Mickey Finn, but its origin is unclear. Bates credits John Alden Knight with making the fly a popular favorite, but not with its creation. Whoever first tied bucktail in alternating yellow, red, yellow over a tinseled hook deserves our thanks for creating a great brook trout seducer.

Lew Oatman's Golden Darter, Charles DeFeo's Black-Nosed Dace, Bill Edsen's Edsen Tiger, and Earl Madsen's Buzz Saw are specific examples of patterns that were (and under certain conditions still are) highly successful. The Black-Nosed Dace remains in wide use and frankly deserves its continuing popularity as one of the most productive trout streamers ever developed.

There are, among the "series" of streamer patterns, four sets that deserve special recognition. Sam Slaymaker II developed the Little Trout series based on close scrutiny of small brook, brown, and rainbow trout. These bucktail patterns appeal to the cannibalistic nature of large trout and are highly effective. Keith Fulsher's unique tying method for the Thunder Creek series produces a trim, almost sparse dressing for realistic baitfish imitations. Joe Brooks, certainly one of our sport's most revered personalities, adapted a tarpon fly and subsequently popularized the Blonde series as magnum bucktails for huge trout. Kelly Galloup has made a few minor changes to the series that seem to make its flies swim better, but the credit for development goes to Homer Rhode Jr. and, for public awareness, to Joe Brooks.

More recently, Bob Clouser's innovative addition of barbell eyes to slim, streamlined bucktails has given us the Deep Minnow series—a deep-swimming, hook-point-up, and virtually snagproof group of baitfish imitations that are easily adapted to regional color requirements in both fresh- and saltwater venues. Their effectiveness on large trout is beyond question.

The late Dan Bailey of Livingston, Montana, refined Gapen's original Muddler Minnow and, in fact, created the popular standard for its appearance. Another of Bailey's many contributions to streamer fishing was the blend of the best from the Dark Spruce streamer (the wing) with the deer hair head from the Muddler. This combination, tied over a cream wool body, produces a natural, dark, barred coloration for the back, head, and sides over a pale underbelly. This is the Spuddler, and it is an effective pattern, particularly in the tumbling, high-gradient streams of the Rocky Mountains.

Chester Marion, a Livingston guide, produced blends of different-colored marabou for the wing behind a clipped deer hair head; his resulting multicolored Marabou Muddlers are used throughout the world.

Al Troth, Ed Shenk, James Bashline, Ray Bergman, Joseph Bates Jr., Roderick Haig-Brown, Al McClane, Lefty Kreh, and a score of others have made major contributions in streamer-fly design, in technique, or in the accurate reporting of both. But in our opinion, the most significant design developments in baitfish imitations—those that impact our success today and will continue to influence the future—have come from Dave Whitlock.

Many anglers think of Whitlock's work as regional, big flies representing large prey items for western or Rocky Mountain waters. And they are big. The Whitlock's Sculpin dressing suggests a 3X-long, 2X-stout hook in sizes 1/0, 2, and 4. But in addition to bulk, the fly is designed to swim properly; it has true colors and shape, too, along with such realistic and defining features as pectoral fins.

Whitlock recognized that even the trout in brawling western waters were becoming pressured and more selective. The bigger the fish, the more demanding the specifications for a morsel that looks and acts alive—even in Montana and Argentina. His big "western" flies produce in the Beaverkill and the Au Sable as well as the Madison and Yellowstone. We suspect Dave's work will continue to be a major influence well into the new century.

~

The evolution of pattern and technique began with primitive barbs and was accelerated by iron and steel hooks. From ancient man's first hungry attempts to Dave Whitlock's modern analytic design, streamer-fly fishing has continued to evolve. Rods, reels, lines, and leaders comprise our delivery system and are vastly superior today than the very best available to us just a few years ago. We have a wider range of material and hook choices with which to construct our critically designed and hopefully seductive patterns. Our support system—the boats, tubes, vests, waders, and clothing—improves in performance each year. And we see continuing development of strategies and techniques based on a more thorough understanding of trout behavior. We are in a position, thanks to the thoughtful efforts of the past, to put the whole package together and tailor our flies, equipment, and tactics to the pursuit of trophy trout.

# chapter two

# The Behavior of Large Trout

The first time an alevin or "swim-up" darts and hides among the bits of rubble and gravel at the bottom of the stream, it carries with it a yolk sac, its nourishment. By the time it becomes a fry, the yolk sac has been absorbed and the fish feeds on the smallest prey in the food chain—tiny larvae. As a fingerling it can devour larger organisms, such as nymphs and the adult forms of caddis, mayflies, and stoneflies. As it grows toward adult status, the young trout consumes larger and larger prey, concentrating on food sources that present the most food value for energy expended.

From the fingerling stage through the early phases of adulthood, feeding trout position themselves strategically. They identify drift lanes that bring the food to them, yet they stay close to cover so they can escape a predator's attack. As growth continues through early adulthood, their range of safety, and therefore their territory, expands to deeper water and to more prominent drift lanes.

At about the time the fish reaches 13 inches in length, its need for nourishment with the least amount of expended energy and risk continues, but because of its increased size it begins an irrevocable turn to larger prey. It becomes a forager, a hunting predator, and as such it has no primary feeding lane. A big fish may move into a feeding lane during a heavy hatch or spinner fall of large insects, but it does not live there. As a trout approaches 16 inches in length it's reaching a stage of dominance, or near-dominance, in the system. It has no need for a position in a feeding lane close to cover; it simply needs a place to rest when it has finished hunting. A dry-fly, wet-fly, or nymph-angler has been conditioned to look for the lines where drifting flies follow natural currents. These are great spots to fish for medium-sized trout, but the real trophies are likely elsewhere.

## Territory

So, where are they? A study conducted by Michele M. De Phillip is of particular interest. The report was submitted to the School of Natural Resources and Environment at the University of Michigan as a Master of Science thesis. It centers on movements of large brown trout (and walleyes) from the Au Sable River's Mio dam downstream to the Alcona dam, a distance in excess of 25 miles.

Eight large browns were implanted with radio transmitters, and their subsequent movements were monitored from May 1996 through the remainder of 1996 and most of 1997. Selected highlights from this report and from previous studies on the Au Sable River include the following: Large brown trout made frequent long-range movements associated with foraging, and this "range of movement increased with fish size due to a shift in foraging strategy from sit-and-wait to active-search . . . Prey density and energetic cost appeared to influence choice of foraging strategy." The studied trout ranged from 44 to 60 cm (17 to 24 inches) in length. The local territory for these trout between May 1996 and August 1997 ranged from just 5 meters to 1,779 meters! Four home ranges were less than 250 meters in length. The studied trout were most active at sunrise and sunset and regularly moved from daytime resting positions (low water volume and current speed) to nighttime feeding positions (higher volume and speed). The complete report contains over 70 pages of valuable information to anyone interested in the behavior, and specifically the movement patterns, of large brown trout.

In recent years several research studies on the movements of large trout have been conducted under strict scientific rules. The results indicate that larger fish establish territories with both daily and seasonal movements attributable to foraging and spawning.

～

On a bright, late-August day in 1997, we both had client cancellations and decided to fish the Au Sable "big water" below Mio. The white fly *(Ephoron leukon)* hatch had begun, and our plan was to fish streamers until dusk then switch over to size 14 duns and spinners until full darkness had settled. Even a large fish will "dial in" to a heavy hatch of hefty-sized bugs, and the white fly, the brown drake *(Ephemera simulans),* and the lead-winged or maroon drake *(Isonychia sadleri)* are the three that most reliably bring big trout to the surface on this section of the river. We knew that the biggest fish of our float would probably come on streamers, but a change of pace is often welcome and dry-fly fishing to slurps in the gloom is great fun.

We pushed off from the boat ramp at the town of Mio about 1 PM. The sky was clear; only a few white puffs layered overhead, and the breeze was soft and intermittent. It was warm, about 85 degrees according to my notes, and the water temperature (at 3:30 PM) was 64 degrees.

Kelly stripped a few feet of line from his reel and knotted a size 2, 4X-long olive Zoo Cougar to his short leader. He had made three casts before the boat cleared the downstream edge of the launch area, and an even dozen by the time we hit the head of the first big pool just 70 to 80 yards below the ramp. Kelly is thorough. Because of the clear sky and water, we thought that the fish would hug the shaded north bank and the gravel ridge at the edge of the drop-off, and we were half right.

Sculpin patterns are the authors' first choice for the large, aggressive brook trout of northern Canada. This fish is a "coaster" caught in a Lake Superior tributary.

Two casts to the bank brought follows; the third produced a rainbow of about 14 inches. Kelly cast again to the bank, then twice to the heavy water at the seam of the drop-off. No pull, no flash, nothing. His next cast was an almost casual flip to the right of the boat, which at this spot was inside the curve on the south side of the river. The fly hit with a heavy splat about 20 feet from the boat and began to sink. We could see the yellow marabou tail flutter once, then straighten as Kelly started his retrieve. On his second strip, a large coppery form rose from the bottom and accelerated toward the fly. As Kelly started his third strip, the trout swarmed over the top and around the Cougar then came straight forward, mouth open, close to the boat—too close. It saw us, stopped the charge, and slowly sank out of sight.

A bit farther down, with Kelly on the oars, we approached a deep, sweeping hole that makes an almost 90-degree turn to the right, then straightens for 40 yards and bends hard to the left. There is a lot of churn and mix to the water in this area, where the river braids around small islands and then dumps back into the main flow. The curves and tailouts at both ends of the S have produced good fish on a more or less regular basis, and we anticipated a hookup in one of the deep slots.

The upstream curve of the S is fed by a bank-to-bank riffle that runs from 1 to 2½ feet deep. The bottom is a mix of cobble, heavy gravel, decayed logs, and sand. The banks are undercut, covered with heavy grass, and tangled with deadfalls. This riffle is about 50 yards long and 75 feet wide. Every pebble on the bottom is visible except after the heaviest rain.

Conventional wisdom (and past experience) predicts strikes in the heavier, deeper water through the curves and in the tailouts under low-light conditions, but this day had already shown us that the larger trout were using a wide range of water types.

Bob was fishing a yellow conehead Marabou Muddler. He sent his first cast close to the north bank then retrieved with a heavy-handed jerk-strip and one-second pauses. The fly darted and swooned, darted and swooned back to the boat, perpendicular to the current flow. Roughly halfway through the second cast, a long form materialized from the bottom and thumped the fly hard. Bob had lost his hold on the fly line at precisely the worst possible moment and could not set the hook. The fish, a brown of about 25 inches, swirled around the fly but would not hit it a second time. Nor did it flee downstream to the deep hole, as we expected. It moved toward the bank, slowly, and just disappeared into the perfect camouflage of the riffle. We pulled the boat to shore and worked Zoo Cougars and Woolly Sculpins through that riffle to no avail. Although we took some smaller fish, both rainbows and browns, throughout the S curves, the big brown did not show again (until much later in the season—but more on that later). We agreed that this was a classic example of territorial defense. The fish wasn't hungry; it had finished hunting and was resting.

∾

The lesson for us was simple: Big trout are wherever they want to be at any given moment. They are not required to hide under tangled log-jams, in undercut banks, at the bottom of the deepest runs and holes. They hunt, they kill and eat, they rest. Kingfishers are no longer a concern, nor are mink. Blue herons are rarely a threat to a really large trout, and although otters are making a comeback, the only consistent danger comes from wading or boating anglers.

Bob releases a hefty brown that attacked a Woolly Sculpin from a flat, featureless tail-out in less than two feet of water.

Like all dominant predators, trophy-sized trout establish a primary territory. The boundaries of this territory will expand or contract based on the availability of food and comfort, and the dominant trout will most likely tolerate other predators within its territory as long as they do not crowd or startle it. A startled or surprised meat eater reacts with aggression. A sleeping dog by the door, a bear or lion dozing near its kill, a large brown trout near the bank—all rely on instinct when suddenly crowded. This instinct is aggression. The dog bristles, growls, and shows its teeth; the grizzly swats the black bear; the lion eats the photographer; and the big brown smashes the streamer. Fight or flight. Attack or be attacked. This instinctive reaction is fundamental to survival and, as such, is irrepressible.

More than a few graduate degrees have been recently awarded, and many more are in process, based on the study of trout and char movements and range boundaries. Various studies scrutinize home-range and foraging strategies, habitat enhancement, defense of exclusive territory by dominance, fish size and system (river) size, nocturnal versus diurnal activity, season of the year, freestone versus limestone stream, spate versus spring creek. It's probably safe to say that any state with a university and a trout stream also has a fair number of trout going about their business with tiny implanted transmitters signaling their every move. The trout and char of Pennsylvania, Maryland, New York, Michigan, Colorado, Idaho, Wyoming, and other states broadcast from lakes, ponds, streams, and rivers of various types—including freestone and limestone, large and small, all with varying degrees of fertility or biomass carrying capacity.

The studies are careful to point out that they report what happened, under what conditions, over a specified period of time. They are not predictive. But if you believe that a trout stays under the same log 22.5 hours out of each day, or that it travels 50 kilometers or 50 meters in a month, you can find a carefully researched, rigorously analyzed scientific study to back you up.

Our nonscientific but experiential data tells us that big trout are less likely to travel significant distances in large, fertile rivers than in smaller, more sterile streams. Except to find access to spawning gravel, fish in a rich environment have little need to roam. But neither do they hang out continually under the same log or undercut bank. Again, there's no need. They seem to go where they want, when they want, without precise predictability. One thing is sure: A trophy trout in a river is one of the system's top predators. It's a big wolf in the pack and has little to fear. It might be holding right where you think it should—at the edge of dark water, near the undercut and behind the log. Cast there. Everybody does. But the fish could just as well be on the far side of the riffle, where it blends sand to gravel and stone, in 2 feet of water. Cast there too. Nobody else will.

## Feeding Patterns

Trout are extremely sensitive to the smallest changes in their environment—weather, light penetration, water flow, temperature, and pressure. Within their territories, large trout are familiar with internal microclimates, or zones, that offer more comfort, security, or easily obtainable food as the overall weather, flow, or time of day changes. Cooling springs, deep shade, rocky tailouts with dense, nocturnal crayfish populations, the soft inside flows of large curving pools under high-water conditions—all are deeply ingrained into a trophy trout's behavioral pattern. With this in mind, we can single out a number of changing conditions that influence a large trout's movements.

The weather (air temperature, water temperature, wind, barometric pressure), available light (time of day or night and cloud cover), and volume of flow (impact of rain or turbine flow) are the most critical factors affecting how often a big fish feeds and where and when he chooses to do so. The water should be in the fish's comfort range—usually 55 to 69 degrees Fahrenheit—or warming toward this in order to spike its metabolic rate and accelerate hunger. Light penetration needs to be low so the fish feels more secure. You need to identify the primary prey species for the water and fish appropriate patterns. You need to find a hungry fish. Pretty restrictive.

All of this is modified somewhat by the relative fertility of the river. If the river is rich in food, the fish are pickier. Simple.

As a good example, let's look at the Manistee River in the northwestern quadrant of Michigan's Lower Peninsula. For much of its run to Lake Michigan, the Manistee's streambed is a thin layer of frosting on top of an aquifer called the Antrim aquifer system. Throughout the river's course it is fed and cooled by countless springs that push groundwater through the thin crust. The Manistee's flow is stable and fertile. Add to this glowing profile two power-generating dams, and you have a spring creek (one of the five largest ground-spring rivers in North America) that is also a tailwater fishery. This makes for well-fed trout that grow to impressive size. The "well-fed" part allows them to be critical and picky, which makes them seem (almost) lazy and arrogant.

As the browns and rainbows of the Manistee approach the 16-inch mark they turn more and more to sculpins, juvenile trout, and crayfish as primary food sources. They will, of course, continue to munch on nymphs and surface-feed on occasion, but the bugs must be large, numerous, and easy. And other conditions must be right. For reliable surface-feeding the water temperature needs to be above 54 degrees. Even when all of these variables come together to provide optimum dry-fly fishing, the large trout will be actively feeding on insects for a very short period. Over 24 hours, the amount of time that a trout over 16 inches spends feeding on the surface in most rivers—even under ideal conditions—is very limited. A trophy trout is much more likely to stalk and eat a fish feeding on mayflies or caddis than to spend its energy feeding directly on the insects. Most of all, these larger trout actively seek out sculpins and crayfish. They show a marked preference for low-light activity when hunger is the primary motivator.

We have been long taught that big trout, particularly brown trout, are strictly nocturnal feeders. This teaching is wrong. We have also been told that they are strictly piscivorous—eating only other fish. This is also incorrect. All large trout and char will feed during the day if conditions so move them—high, discolored water, for instance, and heavy cloud cover. And as opportunists, they will also chew on mice, small birds, frogs, salamanders, snakes, earthworms—you name it.

But to fish successfully for trophies by appealing to their hunger you must key into both their primary feeding cycles, in terms of time and weather conditions, and their primary prey. Typically—and whether you are fishing the Beaverkill, the Delaware, the Au Sable, the Madison, or the Snake—this means you are fishing at dawn, at dusk, or in the night, under heavy clouds and maybe in high water, and that you are throwing sculpin, other baitfish, or crayfish patterns.

## Aggression versus Hunger

The fundamental motivators that fire the synapse that causes a trout to strike, or eat a fly, are but two—aggressive instinct and hunger. What patterns you select, where you cast them, and how you manipulate their movement through the water directly affect whether a trout's response is triggered by instinctive aggression or by the need to eat to survive.

Comparatively speaking, all cold-blooded animals, including trout, need to eat less frequently than warm-blooded animals. As temperatures rise to a trout's "ideal" range, its metabolism peaks, it becomes more active, and its need for food—its hunger—rises accordingly. But how much time does a large trout actually spend hunting and eating as opposed to resting? You can assume that a trout over 20 inches is relatively efficient in obtaining maximum food with minimum energy. How much time does it take to gather several crayfish, to whack a few sculpins, to stalk and eat a smaller trout? Maybe a few minutes, perhaps an hour, possibly two hours? Of course this varies by river; by water volume from rainfall, snowmelt, or turbine discharge; by temperature; and by pure circumstance. Still, even if we assign 4 hours each day to hunger satisfaction, this leaves 18 hours, or 75 percent of each 24-hour period, for rest.

Let's assume that a stretch of river supports 100 trophy trout, a mix of browns and rainbows, ranging from 20 to 28 inches. Because most of these fish are inclined to hunt and eat under low-light conditions or at night—and because most of us fish during the day—it is dead-solid certain that less than 30 percent of these trophies will be hungry, actively focused on food, during the average wade or float trip.

Even at rest with a bulging stomach, a large trout remains alert and active. Its survival instinct dictates constant surveillance of its immediate surroundings, a vigilance tuned to intruders. Threatened with the likelihood of a nose-to-nose confrontation with an otter, any trout will flee, but it is difficult to frighten an alpha with a 4-inch sculpin pattern. An intruder that is also a prey species—trout, sculpin, dace, or darter—is almost always rushed and attacked if it behaves normally. A 3-inch brook trout knows it has made a serious mistake if it finds itself too

Kelly carefully lifts a magnificent Dean River steelhead. It ate a large olive Madonna.

close to a 20-inch rainbow. As soon as it recognizes the mistake, it behaves predictably—a panic move out of harm's way. The little trout swims hard and fast away from danger. Your fly should mimic this movement. The aggressive nature of the large fish asserts itself, the territorial-defense synapse fires, a charge and—most often—a punishing grab, follow. The fish cannot resist this critical, instinctive reaction. It will decline food if full, but it is absolutely programmed to fight or flee if threatened. The trout we target are not frightened by streamer patterns. If they flee, it's because they've been intimidated by the angler or the boat.

## Food Sources

Kelly's synthetic reproduction mounts of trout and steelhead are glistening, seemingly alive, ready to dash to dark water. Before replica mounts became popular, Kelly, as a taxidermist, gained a tremendous insight into the food preferences of large trout by the simple weight of numbers; he autopsied hundreds of them. "Fins, fur, claws, webbed feet; that's what's in their stomachs 99 percent of the time," he states flatly.

**Sculpins**  A significant percentage of those fins are attached to sculpins. Sculpins belong to the family Cottidae and inhabit both fresh and salt water. There are over 80 species of sculpins in North America, ranging in size from 2 inches to more than 30 for some saltwater spec-

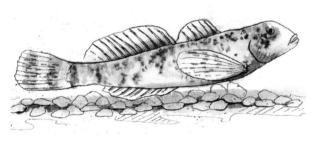

Sculpins are one of the most widespread and preferred foods of trophy trout.

imens. Sculpins are immediately recognizable by their broad, flat heads, which seems disproportionately large for their bodies (see illustration), as well as their large pectoral fins. The species of most interest to fly-anglers include the mottled and slimy sculpins in the 2- to 4-inch range. Look for sculpins in trout streams with stretches of rock, cobble, and coarse gravel. They typically prefer to dwell close to the bottom, using the stones for cover. Their swimming motion is erratic—short bursts of 6 to 12 inches each, followed by a pause—nearly always on or very near the bottom, with the pause usually coming in the shelter of cover. They are rich in protein and are relatively weak swimmers, making them a preferred item on the trout's menu.

**Darters** Darters belong to the perch family, Percidae. Their primary range is the eastern United States, but they also range across southern Canada. Like sculpins, darters try to hide among the bottom rocks and gravel, but they are much faster swimmers and move in short, dartlike bursts—

Darters are strong swimmers. The imitations should be fished in quick, erratic bursts.

hence their name. They are smaller and much harder for a trout to catch than sculpins, and so are not as significant a food source. However, they are widely distributed in most cold-water streams and large rivers, and should not be ignored. Two to 3 inches is about maximum length for an effective darter pattern.

**Dace** Dace (*Rhinichthys* spp.), are widely distributed throughout the United States and Canada. They insist on cold, clear water and seem to prefer streams with cobble, gravel, and undercut banks for cover, although some dace are found in clean, cool lakes. They are not particularly strong swimmers and are a favorite prey (and bait) species in

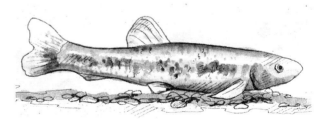

Dace require the same cold, oxygen-rich environment as trout. Dace patterns are most popular in the eastern United States and Canada.

the waters they inhabit. The blacknose dace is a favorite trout food in the central and eastern sections of the Western Hemisphere, and there are numerous effective fly patterns up to 4 inches in length to represent this minnow.

**Shiners**   Shiners (*Notropis* spp.), as a prey species for trout, are most often found in slower, slightly warmer streams than darters and dace. They are found throughout the United States and south-

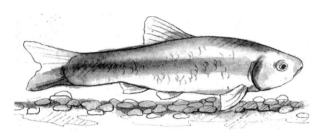

ern Canada. In cool, swift streams they are most likely to congregate in the slower pools. They range in size from 2 to 5-plus inches and are a favorite prey of large trout in certain waters. The Namekagon River in northern Wisconsin has a thriving shiner population as well as some very large brown trout. A Golden Shiner streamer is one of the most effective patterns for trout in this river.

Found most often in slightly warmer flows, shiners are a common prey item for large brown trout.

**Other Trout**   Trout will, of course, quickly cannibalize smaller trout whenever the opportunity is presented. We usually think of trout streamer patterns as relatively small—imitating fry and fingerlings—but trout do not become immune to attack until they are much larger than any fly you can realistically cast and fish.

Rainbow trout, ranging from 6 to 8 inches, are planted right after the Memorial Day weekend at selected access points in a river in northern Michigan. Hundreds of these hatchery fish are dumped into the flow where they will be easy to catch, and they quickly become forage for the huge brown trout that congregate in the deep water just downstream. Local anglers and knowledgeable tourists throw 5- and 6-inch streamers tied to represent the little rainbows. Streamers tied with white rabbit hair strips, a few strands of red or pink Krystal Flash, and large eyes attract browns in the high-20-inch category throughout the month of June. Even when fish that are normally regarded as respectable—say 12 inches and up—zero in on major hatches of mayflies, stoneflies, and caddis, the really big trout are zeroing in on them.

Two years ago we were timing the feeding pattern of a medium-sized trout during the *Hexagenia limbata* hatch on the Au Sable above the small town of Mio. It was about 10 PM and still light enough to see. (Michigan is at the western edge of the eastern time zone; full darkness does not occur until roughly 10:20 in late June.) This fish was charging left and right to suck down large spinners; it was clearly focused on this first wave of bugs floating into its "zone" from farther upstream. Our questions on timing were centered as much on *where* to cast as on *when*. After some analysis and guesswork we made two, perhaps three, casts . . . when a huge, plungerlike boil erupted right about where we thought our riser should be positioned. In addition to the surge and sound of the kill, we saw a slab of gold maybe 7 seven inches across and well over 2 feet long. There is no way we can know for sure, but we guessed that our careless riser was 12 to 14 inches long. It had been stalked and eaten just as surely as if it had been a 4-inch sculpin.

**Crayfish** Crayfish are of the order Decapoda, which means "10 legs." They are common in freshwater lakes and streams throughout North and South America and Europe, and are a favorite trout food. The crayfish—also called crawdads, crawfish, and mudbugs—of interest to fly-anglers range in size from 1

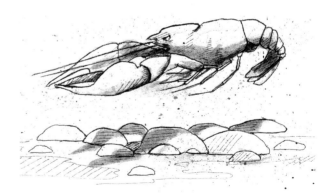

As this illustration shows, the claws fold into each other and appear "streamlined" when a crayfish is fleeing danger.

to 4 inches and in color from orangish tan to a dark olive, almost black on the top, with a creamy underbelly. Low, warm water will often put trout off their normal fare, but a crayfish pattern fished deep with short erratic hops along the bottom is almost always tempting.

∾

On the Madison River you'll find a long, sweeping pool above an island a mile or so above Varney Bridge. It is the first serious pool for quite a distance in either direction and hosts a good number of browns, rainbows, and magnum whitefish. It is usually fished with dry flies; deer hair caddis or Trudes are the first choice, followed by nymphs, and, occasionally, streamers.

A few years ago, a friend of ours got married on the shores of Hebgen Lake with the reception immediately following. We remembered that hardhats were in order for the festivities and the ensuing ruckus scattered the locals (grizz included, we speculated) to safer territory. The next day we were lucky to manage even a late start on the Madison, and by the time we reached the above-mentioned pool it was baking hot and midafternoon. We fumbled about and caught a few whitefish on dry flies, and maybe a small rainbow or two on black stonefly nymphs. We lounged on the bank, drank lots of water, and waited for the cooling evening.

Tired jokes and some spooky flashbacks to the reception drove us to the boat, where we began an aimless rummage through our gear bag. We found an extra spool with a full-sinking class V line and decided, more for escape than anything else, to rig up for streamers. It took longer than normal, but eventually the rod was relined and we waded out to crotch depth for a few casts. First, Bob tried a Spuddler pattern— a big one—then a white marabou, followed by a black Woolly Bugger, with not even a hint of interest. No bump, no pull, no flash behind the fly. Nothing.

We were tired and hot and our head hurt. Sweat was getting into our eyes. It would clearly be too much of an intellectual challenge to change our reel spools back to floating lines, so we decided to try a crayfish pattern that had always performed back home in Michigan. Bob's first cast puddled down about 20 feet in front of him and swept downstream to the hoots and jeers of our bank-squatting compadres. "Just missed your ear! Get a helmet!" His second cast was better, a lot better, and the commentary faded to a low mutter.

Bob's intent was to slowly twitch and skip the fly across the current, but the fish ate on his first short strip. It ran straight downstream toward the island with heavy speed. Bob's rod bowed with as much pressure as he dared apply, and the reel handle blurred. The fish just kept going—through the shallow tailout, into the slot to the left of the island, to and through the end of my backing. Bob could not move fast enough to keep up. Good-bye trout, adios crayfish.

There were three more crayfish in my box and my companions—who'd taken a sudden interest in the fishing—and I each caught one trout apiece in the next hour or so. They were not monster fish by any means. Still, a 16-inch brown and two 15-inch rainbows on an otherwise luckless day were more than welcome.

Crayfish are most active at night, but good copies are effective searching patterns throughout the day when fished deep and methodically among the rocks and stream-bottom debris. They need to be skipped and rested, hopped and paused *on the bottom*—not a foot or two up in the water column. Even with a heavy, full-sinking line, additional weight in the form of barbell eyes is frequently necessary to fish these patterns properly.

**Leeches, Lampreys, and Worms** These creatures are important food sources in most, if not all, trout streams. Our personal experiences, as well as observations shared with us by other

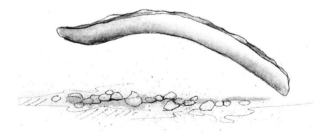

Leeches, lampreys, and worms share the same general shape. Simple ties like the Woolly Bugger can, in different colors, effectively represent all three.

anglers, suggest that they are eaten more as opportunity presents itself than as prey that is specifically targeted and hunted.

Leeches are of the class Hirudinea. They are segmented, parasitic, aquatic worms that attach to their host and suck blood. They are typically 1 to 4 inches in length and vary in color from dark brownish olive to nearly black. They are common throughout North America and are an important food source for many gamefish.

Lampreys feed on fish by attaching themselves with a mouth designed as a combination bore and suction cup. Both adult sea lampreys *(Petromyzon marinus)* and adult silver lampreys *(Ichthyomyzon unicuspis)* are a threat to trout populations in the waters where they occur; specifically, the salmonid populations in the Great Lakes were once nearly eradicated by the intruding sea lamprey. They are eel-like in appearance—long and slender. Sea lampreys are typically 2 to 3 feet long and a dark tan or olive in color. The silver lamprey lives in fresh water from the Mississippi to the East Coast. It is much smaller; adults rarely exceed 12 inches in length, and they are also lighter in color than the sea lamprey. Although the adults are a problem for trout, young lampreys are an abundant, if seasonal, food source when they emerge from the spawning gravel, and again when they emerge from mud burrows in the spring. At this time they are about 4 inches in length and a perfect food for trout.

Worms are a favorite food, too. Tiny aquatic worms in the tailwaters of the San Juan, red earthworms in Wisconsin's Kickapoo, giant night crawlers adrift in the Battenkill, any and all will be quickly eaten by hungry trout if the opportunity is presented. Larger worms are a satisfying meal, helpless and easy to catch.

Leeches, lampreys, and worms have been lumped together here because they can be easily represented by similar streamer patterns that effectively mimic the motion, or action, of the live animals in water. Woolly Buggers, along with marabou, fur-strip, and mohair leech patterns, present an undulating, wormlike motion when retrieved in still water and while drifting in moving water. Simple adjustments in color and length allow these flies, the Buggers, dredgers, and leeches, to mimic any of these three important food sources.

～

In order to exploit the behavior characteristics of large trout, you need to fish streamers that are designed to move in the water so that they specifically play in to a predator's instincts. These flies, which will be discussed in detail in chapter 5, need to present the profile and bulk of a natural prey species. Equally important, you need to cast and move them properly. Tactics and techniques that animate a streamer to appeal to both the aggression and the hunger instincts of trophy trout are presented in chapter 4. A streamer that represents a preferred food source is very good. If that same streamer is constructed to quiver and shake, it's even better. If it suddenly appears as an intruder and tries to flee in a panic, it is ideal.

**Top:** *Most of the high-gradient, boulder-strewn rivers of the Rocky Mountains support large numbers of sculpins. This is the Roaring Fork near Carbondale, Colorado.*

**Bottom:** *Large sculpin patterns can be fished with a variety of techniques to entice trophies like this rainbow. The fly swam deeply with the aid of a ram's wool head and barbell eyes.*

Brian O'Keefe

Barry & Cathy Beck

Brian O'Keefe

**Top:** *The Beaverhead near Dillon, Montana is generally regarded as one of the premier trophy trout rivers of the world. Its biggest fish are particularly fond of large streamers.*

**Bottom:** *Eyes attract predators, and barbell eyes sink flies. This eastern brown trout liked the combination on a sculpin pattern.*

Barry & Cathy Beck

Bob Linsenman

*Top:* A size 2 Trick
or Treat crayfish pattern
fooled this large
Michigan brown trout.

***Bottom:*** *A Beaverhead
River trophy caught
and released by Jeff
Watt. His streamside
coach watches carefully.*

Brian O'Keefe

Brian O'Keefe

Bob Linsenman

**Far left:** *This incredible northeastern brook trout ate a black leech pattern. A released trophy forever captured on film.*

**Top:** *Streamers regularly produce the biggest trout regardless of geography. This scene is on the Rio Paloma in Chile.*

**Bottom:** *Bob quickly lifts a male brown in spawning colors. It ate a Zoo Cougar in late September.*

**Top:** *Many small streams are overlooked by streamer anglers. This eastern freestone creek holds large fish.*

**Bottom:** *Looking downstream into the Magic Riffle on the lower Au Sable. This run features undercut banks, a deep center cut with two distinct shelves, logs, and shade.*

Bob Linsenman

Brian O'Keefe

**Top:** *Two anglers, each fishing different colors and sizes, can quickly determine the trout's preferences. Here Kelly is directing his clients to cover a deep cut near the bank.*

**Bottom:** *Alaskan rainbows are greedy consumers of large streamers and seem especially fond of large leech patterns. This trophy's home is the Kulik River.*

*Top:* Cathy Beck holds
a magnificent, Pennsyl-
vania brown for a
quick photograph. This
8-pound trophy took a
Woolly Bugger.

*Bottom:* Streamers pro-
duce throughout
the year. The dredge
technique was a good
choice on this cold day
on Fishing Creek in
Pennsylvania.

Barry & Cathy Beck

Barry & Cathy Beck

# chapter three

# Reading the Water

A major part of the attraction of moving water for anglers is its endless variety. In pursuit of trout we enjoy an infinite series of beautiful vistas, kaleidoscopic colors, and symphonic water songs. Spring creeks, freestone rivers, limestone streams, tailwaters of all sorts, spate rivers, and those streams that are classified as one but seem to turn into another are ever changing, chromatic mysteries.

Because of the separate classifications and the diversified flow-system characteristics we've come up with to describe rivers, it is possible (actually, too easy) to become overly concerned with the type of river you're fishing. We anglers often "pigeonhole" in order to sort and organize information, and this often leads to counterproductive assumptions such as the belief that one type of river (perhaps a spring creek) is best fished with dry flies, another is only for nymphs, and a third (say, a larger freestone flow) is ideal for streamers. Yes, trout may have a tendency to feed more on the surface of one river than another—they may have adapted to a specific food source in a given system—but more often than not really large, trophy trout respond to their instincts as meat-eating predators.

All anglers are guilty of attempts to oversimplify, to tightly classify something that's highly complex. We have often caught ourselves in the pigeonhole mode on classic dry-fly rivers like the Bighorn, Henry's Fork, and LeTort. And these waters do host wonderful hatches that consistently produce active and selective surface-feeding by large numbers of trout. Armed with that foreknowledge, and usually specifically because of it, we travel to these rivers to enjoy the challenges of small dry flies, light tippets, and selective, wary fish. But preconceived notions can be detrimental to success. Just because a river has been stereotyped as "dry-fly water" doesn't mean it's not suitable for streamers. In fact, it may present more opportunities with streamers than with drys.

∾

Mike Craig of Fort Smith, Montana, was the first outfitter on the Bighorn River; he owned Big Horn Anglers for 17 years. He's also a very good friend of ours. Mike knows, perhaps better than anyone, how easy it is for anglers to allow a river's reputation to dictate their angling approach and affect their ultimate success. The Bighorn is, flat out, one of the best dry-fly and nymph rivers in the world. It's a classic tailwater with consistent flows and temperatures, and it's extravagantly rich in aquatic food. Anglers from all over the globe travel to the Bighorn, most for its superb dry-fly fishing. Yet when we asked Mike about his best-ever day on the river, he shocked us by saying it was a fall day during which he fished streamers exclusively. Streamers on the Bighorn, the best dry-fly stream in North America? Who would have guessed?

Many years have passed since Mike first relayed the story, and it's not surprising to hear that now many of the top guides on the Bighorn fish streamers much of the time. During a trip to the river in 1998, Kelly noticed an enormous black Matuka on Mike's kitchen table and asked about it. Mike explained that it was the fly Bob Krumm was doing well with on the lower river. Bob Krumm is one of the most sought-after guides on the Bighorn (for good reason), and if he's using a large streamer, it is not for casting practice.

Our point is that it is most often to your advantage to disregard classifications and to view all rivers from the same perspective. Understand the way water acts when pulled by gravity, and the way trout react to current flow, and you will fish all rivers more effectively.

Why do trout prefer certain stretches of river, different current conditions, and various resting places? Scores of magazine articles have been written to show you where a fish (usually!) lies relative to a rock or log in a river, but rarely does the article explain *why* the fish is there. It has a reason for being in a specific location, though. None of the great fly patterns of the world will entice a trout if you fish them in the wrong places. This chapter is designed to help you better understand how and where a river creates the environment that trophy trout prefer.

All fish live in a dynamic world of hydraulic forces. Large, riverine trout are constantly faced with a changing environment. They attempt

This is Werewolf Bend on the lower Au Sable. It features diverse, hospitable habitat with stable flows, shelves, rocks, logs, and undercuts. It is home to several super trout.

to minimize the dynamics and stabilize the forces of their world by finding the most consistent current flows and resting in them when not actively hunting. The big fish looking for food is less concerned about being in a stable flow, but it will always return to one for rest. Smaller fish—juvenile trout and some forage fish—and crustaceans are less able to contend with heavy, erratic flows and are governed by milder, more stable currents. Consequently, a big trout will regularly leave a stable holding area to search for prey, but smaller fish will not. And like most aggressive predators, this trophy fish will most often hunt early and late in the day. This simplifies matters somewhat for the angler and, if you are like the two of us, simplification is a *good* thing. Understanding that large trout are in a resting state much of the day allows you to stalk stable holding areas rather than attempting to intercept cruising fish.

## The River

In order to effectively analyze a river and its potential big-trout zones, you need to examine several key elements that impact water action or current flow and therefore affect trout behavior. The most critical elements are structures: rocks, logs, weeds, undercut banks, logjams, and shelves. Add to these such considerations as depth, current speed, and fertility and you pretty much know all the key factors that affect fishing on any river in the world.

Flowing water strives for efficiency, and this means a straight-line flow. It constantly works against obstacles—banks, rocks, logs—moving them out of the way with pressure and friction. A river is constantly moving, readjusting and reorganizing itself. About the time you finally figure out a deep, challenging run, a spring flood will wash out the upper half, depositing a mass of willow roots near the inside bank and changing the entire set of hydraulic conditions. All rivers constantly move the pieces of the angling puzzle; sometimes this is a subtle adjustment, but often enough it is a full-tilt scramble. Isn't nature great?

To understand why a trout holds in a particular position in front of

Rock Wilson and Kelly (on the oars) are in position to fish both log structures and an undercut bank.

or behind an obstruction, you need to look at how the water reacts to that obstruction. There is a simple but highly illustrative experiment that takes only a few seconds to perform but will quickly show you how moving water behaves. Place an upright stick in moving water. This requires the current to separate into two flows around the obstruction. Each of these currents is slowed closest to the stick by friction, while outside the water continues at its normal speed. These two separate current speeds create more friction, which in turn creates a hydraulic swirl (*hydraulic* simply means water in motion and the effects of water in motion). The two currents eventually reconverge downstream from the obstruction, creating another hydraulic called a *seam*. This is just one, simple example of how water works. It is the friction between obstructions and varying current speeds that makes up the incredibly diverse conditions of a living river. The complexity is dynamic and challenging—and it certainly helps explain the attraction of moving water.

## Rocks

Rocks are one of the most common obstructions in rivers. The huge boulders of the Green River in Utah, the fist-sized stones of Barnhart's Pool on the Beaverkill, the small and random cobble of the Au Sable's Holy Water—all rocks have a dramatic impact on moving water. We will concern ourselves here with bowling-ball-sized rocks and larger, but even small stones create the same conditions. These smaller obstructions create smaller impact zones that are often ideal holding areas for baitfish and other aquatic life.

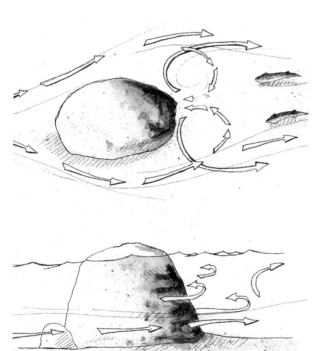

Large rocks create multiple currents. Below the confusion of reverse currents there is always a stable, comfortable holding area for large trout.

Let's start with a close scrutiny of that rock that has appeared in almost every issue of every fly-fishing magazine for the past 30 years. You know the one. It is a fairly large boulder, viewed from the top, and the drawing shows a relatively fast current breaking around it with one or more trout holding below.

As the solid water mass meets the rock's upstream face, it is slowed and split. As the water is pushed backward (upstream) off the face, it is hit by the faster, outside current. This forces the slower current to spin in the opposite direction—back toward the rock—which creates a seam (a seam is created whenever two different currents meet). This happens simultaneously on each side of the rock. When the flows of water from both sides reach the back (downstream side) of the rock, they are turning in opposite directions. When they rejoin, this reverse flow pushes the water back toward the rock. The current that is being pushed back upstream is called a *reverse,* or negative, current. This reversing action, a reaction to friction, is created when differing current speeds meet. And this is the key to understanding the effect of obstructions on hydraulic flow. If you can understand how moving water reacts to a rock, you can figure out just about any situation you are likely to encounter.

The softer, cushioned current behind the rock provides the trout with several favorable conditions. Most important are the seams, which create easy, low-energy places for fish to wait in ambush and watch for prey. Additionally, the seams break up the water's surface, which provides a sense of security from predators. A feeding fish can hold in the soft current with little exertion and view the sweep of food in the faster, outside current. These negative, soft, or reverse currents are the reason we catch trout in water that seems too fast, too rough to hold them. The fish were not holding where they took the fly. They were holding in the soft edge, and attacked into the faster flow. Regardless of how fast the water is flowing, rocks that penetrate the surface or at least rise close to it create softer currents to hold trout.

To fish a rock effectively requires a thorough approach, usually several casts. Occasionally, trout will have their noses tight behind the rock, but more often they will hold in or near the seam where two currents meet. Cast past the downstream side of the rock and retrieve your streamer across both current seams directly behind the rock. Repeat the cast in 1- to 2-foot increments downstream. This allows the fly to come into view naturally from the faster outside current, into the slower seam, then again through the inside current.

## Logs

In our home rivers in Michigan and many other streams throughout the country, logs are the dominant in-stream structures that require analysis and understanding. Few places in the world have been logged as heavily as Michigan; still, the logging industry has left its mark throughout the northern, forested tier of the States and the Canadian provinces. Rivers were this industry's primary mode of transport. The trees were felled, limbed, and skidded to the closest river for the spring run downstream to the mills. Many logs did not make it to the mills; these leftovers, trapped singly or in jams, have created wonderful fish cover. This is particularly true in the Great Lakes basin. We have no mountains, so we seldom receive a spring runoff heavy enough to scour our rivers and clean the wood from the system.

Even rivers with annual, heavy spring flooding trap and hold the occasional deadfall or logjam. Logs can "lock" into a river in a variety of ways, from the perpendicular stab of a single structure into a soft mud bank to a Tinkertoy pile of confusion with root wads, whole trees, and limbs twisting in every direction. Logs that lie perpendicular as well as parallel to the current flow are equally important if you're fishing streamers.

Logs lying perpendicular to the flow create two distinct currents. First, the water that directly impacts the upstream face

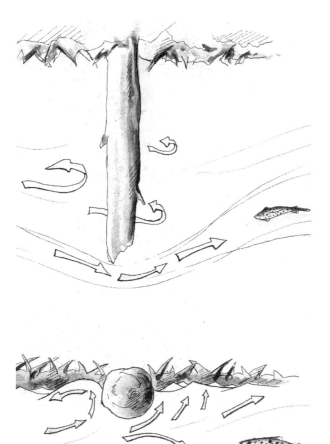

Water directly in front of and behind this log has too much lift. For best results look to the lower outside seam where water is more stable.

of the log backs up to the surface and creates a hump. As the current flowing downstream hits the water backing up, it forces more water to the surface and pushes the middle layer of water toward the bottom. As the water flows under the log, it begins to spin. This is caused by water that has been slowed and pushed downward by friction (from the log) hitting the faster current beneath it. This spins or tumbles the flow in the opposite (upstream) direction.

If one end of a perpendicular log is exposed above, or comes very near, the water's surface, another hydraulic effect comes into play. This is the same dynamic created by a rock. In this situation you'll see compound currents, with water moving, curling, spinning, and creating seams in several directions. If these currents have too much speed and volume, they are generally too unstable to hold fish; the trout most often move away from the confusion toward the softer seams where the currents meet again and stabilize. The hump, or upward bulge of water in front of the log, looks appealing but will rarely hold a trophy-sized fish. Occasionally, you will find small to medium-sized trout surfing the hump for surface flies, but of all the possibilities presented by logs this is the least productive. This is due to a combination of adverse factors. The multiple currents are problematic, but of more significance is the negative impact of hydraulic lift. Big trout do not like lift. This is a bad thing. Water forced toward the surface is uncomfortable, difficult, and dangerous for trout. Their survival instincts direct them elsewhere—to the outside edges of the lift or hump area, to the current seam closest to the bank, and to the primary tailout of the downstream current seam. Fish these areas hard with repeated casts and close attention. A darting, swooning Zoo Cougar or a cream Woolly Sculpin often produces an exciting charge.

Logs that lie with or nearly with the river's flow are *parallel* structures. How such a log is secured, and at which end, dictates its impact on the current. If a log has simply come to rest on the bottom and is partially submerged, it produces little of the hydraulic dynamics that are attractive to trophy trout. This most commonly happens in low to moderate current. Usually a deadfall becomes entangled on the bank or stuck to the bottom by its root wad, which causes the trunk or stem to trail downstream like a rudder. Rarely is the current exactly even on both sides of a parallel log. More dirt and debris build up on one side, and this often produces an interesting result: The log shows a dramatic color change from one side to the other. Whether or not these logs produce a good-sized fish, they always create the anticipation of a heavy strike.

Parallel logs, unlike perpendicular structures, deflect water but do

Small streams and side channels of larger rivers often combine many preferred flow and cover characteristics within a short distance.

not disrupt its flow dramatically. The current is not stopped and pushed backward, only slowed. The result is that much less water is forced down and under the log. With less volume pushing downward, there is less corresponding hydraulic lift to the flow behind or beside the log. Still, the water *is* slowed, and the seam created on the trailing, downstream edge is usually quite soft.

The great setup for the fly-angler is the log structure that is 1 to 3 feet from the bottom and casting shadows. If the top of the log is 6 to 12 inches below the surface, the scenario is ideal. If you find such a structure, it is almost a sure bet that a large trout will be nearby.

The best way to fish such an opportunity is to show your streamer on both sides of the log on each cast. Start on the upstream edge or slightly above and cover the structure with as many casts as necessary to ensure full exposure. Your casts should, if possible, extend at least 2 feet past the far side of the log—farther is better. This allows your streamer to be seen from both sides and will also (if the day is bright) cast a lifelike shadow down to the river's bottom. These structures often have multiple holding and ambush sites, so fish them as thoroughly as possible.

## Logjams—The Ultimate Cover

A large logjam is almost always the best holding and ambush station you will find in any stretch of any river. Logjams occur in infinite variation, so it is impossible to describe them all. But they do have some similarities that we can break down and analyze.

The very nature of a logjam is static havoc born of the wild anarchy of floods. Logs slam into riverbanks, root wads stick to the bottom, with branches and trunks grabbing, holding, and locking into a confused jumble. The logs create hospitable environments for nymphs, crayfish, and baitfish. The mix of sun and shadow, the soft side currents, and the overhead cover created by the jam is the ultimate security blanket for a large trout. And most logjams, especially the really good ones, are found at corners and bends, so you'll generally find the additional benefit of increased water depth.

Logjams are big-trout hotels with a luxurious, ever changing ambience. Every branch and leaf wad that is swept into or out of the structure affects the environment and causes adjustment. This is a good thing for the fish, but because of the enormous, dynamic complexity, jams are not always the most productive zones for strikes. Depending on the complexity of the structure, it is not always possible to place a cast where your quarry can see the fly.

To fish a logjam properly, it is important to pause a few moments and examine the possibilities. Study the hydraulics. Where are the softer current seams? Look especially for logs (perhaps submerged) that are lying parallel to the current. You'll most often need to make multiple presentations to various locations to effectively fish a jam. Give the fish as many chances as possible to see your streamer. Often the water will be quite deep and you may find it difficult to get the fish to ascend from its resting area during midday hours. But the trophies will be checking into and out of these log hotels every dawn and dusk, and for this reason it pays to fish the jams diligently early and late in the day. Patterns that flutter and undulate in twisting currents—conehead Marabou Muddlers, Woolly Sculpins, Madonnas, Strip Leeches and Cougars—produce well in the confused flows of logjams.

## Gradient Changes and Shelves

A logjam may well be the favorite holding spot for large trout, but for anglers they take a distant second place to gradient changes and shelves for overall results. Gradient changes and shelves are the core of any river. Rivers can exist without logs, jams, or boulders, but without a degree of drop (gradient), gravity does not pull and water does not flow. The degree of gradient and the height of the shoulders of a river's channels (creating shelves) constantly change throughout the river's course. We can label these changes as riffles, runs, or chutes, but they are all essentially gradient changes.

Most anglers are inclined to call quick water less than 2 feet deep a *riffle,* and water more than 2 feet deep a *run.* That's good enough. The

gradients you want to be concerned with are those that feature
an uneven surface, caused by an
uneven bottom or by shelves.
An uneven bottom and ragged
shelves are most often found
where the channel bed and surrounding land are very hard or
rocky. A river carves its channels
based on current speed, which is
controlled by the pull of gravity—
gradient change. A shelf is created
at the side of the channel cut, and
often on both sides.

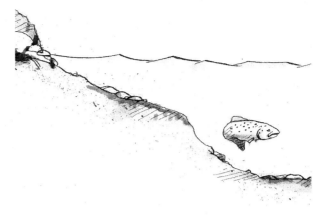

Gradient changes, or shelves, can be very subtle
or deeply grooved and obvious. The key to
identifying them is close scrutiny. These are critical
fish holding areas.

A shelf creates a perfect hy-
draulic nest as well as an ideal ambush point. These two factors make
shelves most attractive to the largest trout in the area. With cushioning
seams, hydraulics that bring prey up close, overhead visibility to screen
for predators, and a parallel color change with depth for additional security, the shelf is perfect habitat for predatory trout.

The current impact of a shelf is easy to understand. As the water
flows into the groove or channel it churns toward the bottom, creating
the slower currents and cushioned pockets that make it easy for a hunter
to rest safely at depth. And as the faster flow washes over the top edge
of the shelf, it brings prey. Regardless of the type of river you fish most
often—freestone, limestone, spring creek, or spate—shelves hold the
most fish per mile.

The primary holding area for trout is (usually) the steepest shelf or
fastest side of the channel, but often enough (and particularly after a
rain) we have found that the dominant predator trout will take up an
ambush station on the slower side of the channel. The increased volume
of water moves plenty of food to it, and its energy output is greatly re-
duced here on the "soft side." Under normal flows, the faster current on

the steep side of the shelf delivers a reasonable volume of food in relation to the energy required for the trout to station there. An abnormally heavy flow calls for too much work.

As guides, we field a lot of questions. One of the most common is "Where do you look for large fish?" "In the water" is a standard reply, but the unamused client then receives a more thorough breakdown. We direct clients to look for parallel color changes in the water. These occur where water depths merge or two bottom types meet. These unions, be they depths or bottom types, dictate a color and shade change and often create a shelf. Additionally, a current seam is usually present, but it is not as readily apparent as the color change. Many shelves are not easily identified, because they do not always feature an abrupt and distinct change in color. This is why, in our opinion, shelves are the most consistently overlooked hot spots in a river system.

It is difficult to find a gradient change that hasn't produced a shelf; conversely, it is equally hard to locate a shelf unattended by gradient change. A large hole where the water moves slowly qualifies, and this is easy enough to identify. As a general rule such holes tend to be less attractive to fish unless there are additional factors, such as logjams, present. But these deep, slow, dark, soft-bottomed holes are difficult to resist; they just look good! Try a few casts and concentrate on the tailout at the downstream edge where the depth gradually increases.

Water moving through a sudden gradient change cannot all progress at the same velocity. As an example, let's analyze a chute's angling potential by examining its parts. Water flowing at the edge of the river is slowed by the friction created by contact with the bank. Thus, the friction creates slow water and, where it is met by a faster current, a seam. The fastest part of the current will cut a deeper slot, which will be shouldered by shelves. The slot and shelves can range in depth from several inches to several feet, depending on the water's volume, its velocity, and the bottom's texture. Wherever there are two or more varying water depths, there are corresponding variations in water speed. These

This angler is fishing the deep side of a shelf. He's standing at an obvious color change where the shelf begins to drop off.

different current speeds create hydraulic turmoil and seams. The rocks on the bottom, visible or not, provide additional current breaks and seams. This is an area with tremendous potential for a big-trout hookup, but all of this potential will probably not be visible at first glance. It pays to carefully dissect a fast section of the river. Look for current seams and hydraulic swirls created by hidden rocks and shelves. If you identify the holding and ambush sites, you can fish these areas with great confidence. Remember that small baitfish cannot fight the heavy current; they prefer to stay in the slower edges. These edges and seams are therefore prime ambush locations for predatory trout.

All of this water is being supercharged with oxygen throughout the chute, run, or riffle. It generally offers a high degree of concealment from airborne predators and is rich in aquatic life. Still, many (most) fly-anglers pass it by, or make only one or two token casts. Some anglers do not like to wade heavy currents even under ideal conditions, and we do not encourage any of you to tread beyond your personal comfort level. But we hope you at least consider fishing the tailouts of these runs and chutes early and late in the day. These tailouts are rich in nymphs, which draw small fish like a magnet. Large fish often drop back from the heavier current, or migrate upstream, to hunt the smaller trout on these flats under low-light conditions.

It is our opinion that shelves are the most underfished areas in a river. Seldom are they as blatantly obvious as riffles, runs, logs, or rocks. Often they are created by the carving effects of current, but not always; sometimes they result from geological forces adjusting and shifting differing degrees of hardness, weight, and density in the area's land mass. However created, though, they are usually widespread and common throughout a river's course. And they are major holding areas for substantial trout.

Because they rarely feature a corresponding structure as an identifier, shelves are the easiest to overlook, or flat-out miss, of all the key big-fish hot zones. They often are very close to shore; some may be at the center of the river, but they are *always* present. It is our belief that the main difference between an average angler and a highly successful angler is the ability to detect shelves. Most folks can easily identify the holding and ambush sites of more obvious structures, but locating and covering a subtle shelf is the signature of experience and skill.

A streamer pattern that has produced exceptional results along shelves is the Rattlesnake in various colors. Additionally, Zoo Cougars, Strip Leeches, Woolly Buggers, and conehead Marabou Muddlers are dynamite. When shelf currents are particularly heavy, the yellow Butt Monkey, developed by Ontario angler Scott Smith, will knock their fins off.

## Depth

Pure depth, with or without structure, can create holding areas for large trout. The question confronting most anglers is what constitutes the dividing line between effective, fishable depth and too much of a good thing. At what depth does the pure effort of sinking and effectively moving the streamer outweigh the benefit? This question can only be answered by each individual angler. What we find is that in the waters we fish most often, trout holding deeper than 8 feet require substantial energy and persistence to move. For us, they're seldom worth the effort.

One of the main attractions of streamer fishing (to us) is its visual dimension. The charge of a big trout through a clear riffle, its rush to the surface, its openmouthed slam near a bank are all catalysts for an adrenaline surge. But this is personal opinion. Fishing much deeper than 8 feet requires heavier lines and dredging or backdrifting techniques that virtually eliminate the thrill of a visual take. Still, they are effective enough in certain rivers to merit consideration.

Scott Smith and Bill Boote of Thunder Bay, Ontario, regularly fish the Nipigon River's deepest cuts and holes with Teeny lines. The massive brook trout in the Nipigon often hold very deep under clear skies, but their incredible size, fighting power, and glorious color make the extra effort it takes to pursue them well worthwhile. Our friends' favorite pattern for this deep work on the Nipigon is an olive Strip Leech of considerable proportion. Another pattern that produces well when slithered through the depths is a recent development by Rock Wilson. Rock is the manager of Kelly's fly shop in Traverse City and a creative tyer. His pattern, the Silver Fox, stirs the really big trout to action.

## Undercut Banks

These are usually excellent hideouts for large trout. We say "usually" because the attraction of an undercut bank to a trophy fish is directly impacted by several elements. The character of the surrounding water is

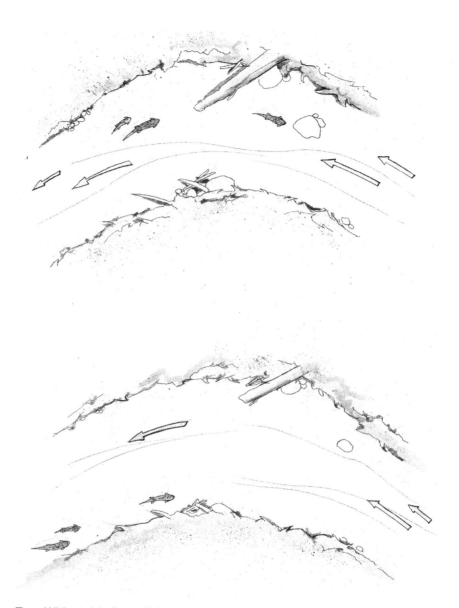

**Top:** With stable flows fish congregate at the outside of bends where there is more volume, flow, and depth. **Bottom:** During high water flows, big fish often move to the inside of bends. The increased water volume adds security and stability for smaller trout and baitfish as well as the large trout.

critical. The depth of the undercut (how *far* the water flows back under the bank), the depth of the water, current speed, and other nearby structures are also determining factors in a given undercut's suitability.

If the bank is undercut from just a few inches to perhaps 2 feet, it is ideal. Trout have overhead cover for security, and an ambush point provides access to terrestrial prey as well as current-borne aquatic food. Undercuts that penetrate more than 2 feet under the bank are usually overly tangled with snags, while undercuts of less than, say, 6 inches provide minimal security and are likely to become unusable, or at least much less attractive, under low-water conditions.

If an undercut is in close proximity to a chute, run, shelf, or logjam, it is unlikely to be the favorite holding area for a dominant predator. But if it is part of a deep hole, a sweeping, featureless curve, or a flat pool, it is likely the best place to fish in the immediate area.

Our favorite time and place to fish undercuts is after (or during) a moderate rain when the river has risen slightly, and specifically at the soft *inside* of a large, deep curve or bend in the river. Big trout are lazy and do

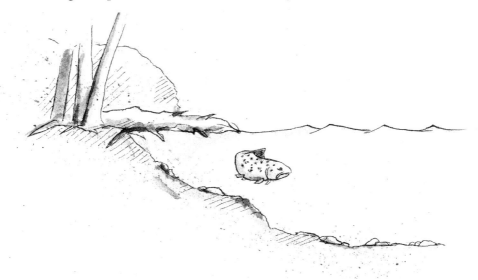

Undercut banks are extremely good holding areas. They offer the ultimate in protection and are extremely productive under high sun conditions.

This undercut bank has two distinct sections. The upper, whitewater stretch has a high velocity flow and is saturated with heavy tangles. The big fish are in the lower section where the current slows.

not like to work any harder than absolutely necessary for their room and board. When the river rises, the current strengthens and usually colors a bit. The inside curves bring a plenitude of food due to the increased flow, but are still moderate and comfortable. The tinge of color adds a sense of security from predators, and the proximity of an undercut provides complete safety. Thus, the big trout fins lazily in the banquet room.

Black, dark brown, and dark olive streamers with just a hint of flash are ideal under these conditions. Slap a large black-winged, pearl-bodied Zonker or an olive Matuka near the undercut and hang on.

## Weed Channels

When I visualize spring creeks like the LeTort, Falling Spring Run, De Puy's, or Nelson's, I rarely think of streamers. The graceful, placid flows bring to mind tiny mayflies, terrestrials, or perhaps sow bugs fastened to long, delicate leaders. I remember (or dream of) a large rainbow lying in a narrow channel partially hidden by the undulating cress. My slack-line presentation drifts the size 22 PMD over the line; the large head breaks the surface and inhales. I tighten carefully and the big trout turns and slams violently to its left, burrowing into the weeds and snapping the tippet. Game over.

This is not just a dream. It happens every day from coast to coast, and it is high sport and extravagant fun. Spring creeks produce very large fish due to the variety and richness of their supporting aquatic food forms. But not all of these food sources are caddis, mayflies, and freshwater shrimp. Spring creeks also support baitfish, crayfish, and leeches in wild abundance. And that large rainbow did not grow to trophy size on a strict diet of pale morning duns or blue-winged olives. It grew and now sustains itself on larger prey.

Pennsylvanian angler Ed Shenk is famous for his incredible success with huge brown trout on streamers in the gentle, smallish spring creeks of the Keystone State. Jac Ford guides in Paradise Valley, Montana, and he too knows that the biggest fish in creeks can best be fooled by a streamer on a stout leader.

In addition to all the structures we mentioned earlier in this chapter, spring creeks usually feature extensive weed beds rich in nymphs, shrimp, snails, leeches, and baitfish. Indeed, the weeds are ideal for small aquatic life. They feature cover, protein, oxygen, and current seams. These attractive features also bring the hunters.

Think of a channel in the weeds as a mini-chute or run. The current at the edges is slowed by friction, providing comfortable ambush, and the overhead screen of the weeds produces total security from overhead danger.

∼

There are obviously countless currents, seams, and structures in every river. They present endless opportunity and variety in terms of angling potential. Sometimes you can be overwhelmed by the magnitude of possibilities, but this can be countered.

Big trout can be anywhere they want to be at any given moment, but you never have enough time or energy to fish every cubic foot of water. By breaking the wide potential into smaller segments, though, you can learn to identify *primary* hot zones and so fish more systematically.

The most important element in reading water is practiced observation. Do not look at a sizable stretch of river as a whole; take the time to break it into smaller, manageable sections. Practice with a 10-foot-long piece. Concentrate on identifying side currents and seams. Look for color changes. Try to determine the location of primary holding water, the distinction between softer hydraulics and pushy, volatile currents. Buy a good pair of polarized glasses. Train yourself to see *into* and *through* the water. Look for color changes. Watch floating debris as it is swept over, around, and under various structures. If you want to be really thorough, buy a mask and a pair of fins and get down in there with the fish. Kelly does this quite often, to his friend's amusement, who think blue is a hilarious skin color.

# chapter four

# Mastering the Techniques

Often associated with off-hatch periods and regarded as an alternative or backup method when fish are not actively surface-feeding, streamers have generally been relegated to the second string. The most widely applied streamer technique is an across-and-slightly-downstream cast followed by a down-and-across swing. It's a passive approach: You cast a minnow pattern, let it swing through large sections of water, and hope there is a hungry trout in the area.

If executed properly, this traditional method swing can produce respectable results with any small to medium-sized fish holding in feeding lanes waiting for food. It has been moderately successful for larger trout as well, but is rarely a first choice by most successful streamer anglers. Although it has accounted for many large fish over the years, it is generally employed with a search-and-hope attitude. A trophy-sized trout taken on a streamer has long been regarded as a great bonus, usually a gift, but certainly not expected.

Since we have adapted our thought process on streamer fishing, however, applying new techniques and a more calculated approach, we have found that the capture of a trophy fish—once an exceptional and rare event—is now common. What was rare is now the norm for us! To excite large trout and make them come to your fly, you too must rethink your approach and very likely modify your equipment selection. In the following pages we will present alternative methods and discuss varying line options that will greatly increase your success with the largest fish in the river.

## Casting Streamers

Effective streamers for trophy trout are generally big flies—much bigger than the nymphs, wet flies, and surface patterns most anglers use on a regular basis. And for ultimate efficiency in almost all situations, we use sinking lines. Sinking-tips, including the Teeny-style, and full-sinking lines simply push the odds in our favor. We use full-sinking lines for about 90 percent of our personal angling and encourage our clients to do likewise.

Many anglers are concerned that they will not be able to cast a sinking line—particularly not a full-sinker. This is true for only one reason: They have never tried it. The fact is, casting a sinking line is no different than casting a floating line, but there are a couple of things to remember that will increase your efficiency.

The actual casting strokes—both your backcast and your forward delivery—are the same as you use with a floating line. The most notable difference in the process is that the sinking line is heavier in relation to its diameter and loads the rod much faster. A few practice casts is usually all it takes for most anglers to become comfortable and even to acknowledge that the sinking line is actually easier to cast than a floater.

The *pickup* is the most important aspect of casting a sinking line. The line must be at or near the surface of the water for an efficient pickup and backcast. To achieve this you have two basic options. First, you can continue your retrieve until the butt of the leader is 20 feet or

**Left:** On the backcast, the rod must pause long enough to allow the line to straighten. **Right:** Push through the cast and stop abruptly. This will propel your cast with extreme accuracy.

less from your rod tip before you attempt to lift the line (the pickup) from the water for the start of your backcast. Lift with a strong, sharp, up-and-back motion to drive the line and fly high behind you. The second option is the *roll-cast pickup*. This is simply a forward roll cast that you use to bring the line onto the surface of the water in preparation for your backcast. It's especially effective with very heavy, long sinking-tips. We use this most often with Teeny-type lines after we've retrieved the fly to within 20 or 30 feet of the rod tip. (This distance is dependent on the length of the sinking forward portion of the line.) An easy way to make the roll-cast pickup almost automatic is to retrieve until the color change (the point of the line where the sinking-tip section meets the floating section) is within an inch or two of your rod tip.

To execute the roll-cast pickup, make an *aggressive* forward roll cast, stopping the rod's drive at 10 o'clock. When the line rolls over and lands on the surface, *immediately* pick up and start your backcast. It is critical to this maneuver that you not let the line sink before you begin your backcast. If the line starts to sink, it will overload the rod on the backcast: It takes all the rod's power to bring the line to the surface, leaving nothing to propel the line behind you. With either the straight-line pickup or the roll-cast pickup, it is imperative that you start with your rod tip low to the water.

Once your backcast is in motion and moving behind you, do not let the line fall toward the water. These are heavy lines with small diameters, and gravity takes over very quickly. If you pause too long before starting your forward power stroke, the line will drop rapidly. If you begin the forward cast after your line has dropped below your rod tip, you may find a large fly impaled in your scalp. The good news is that because of the line's weight and density, you can easily feel and recognize your rod loading, so it's pretty easy to time your forward cast.

The forward cast should be very crisp through the power stroke. Stop the delivery when your rod reaches 10 o'clock. Practice—just a little—and this will quickly become instinctive.

Casting a full-sinking or sinking-tip line does not require a lot of false casts. The line loads the rod with great efficiency, so you should be able to shoot all the line you need with a maximum of one false cast. With practice, you will find it is rarely necessary to backcast more than once per delivery.

## The Jerk-Strip Retrieve

If we could use only one method of streamer fishing for any fish anyplace, the jerk-strip retrieve would be our choice, because it consistently produces large fish and generates excitement. This technique gives you the rewarding feeling of having successfully hunted, located, then moved your fly so as to trigger a response from the fish. It will bring out your primal instincts and will keep your eyes glued to the fly throughout the retrieve. When properly executed, the jerk-strip method

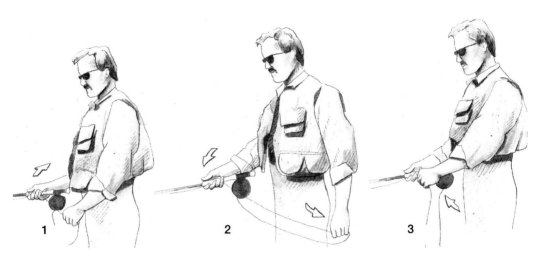

**1.** Start the retrieve with your rod tip pointed at the fly. Jerk the rod downstream 12 to 24 inches. The rod moves the fly; not the line hand. **2.** While returning the rod to the starting position, strip the excess line created by the rod jerk. **3.** Quickly return line hand to starting position and repeat.

triggers aggressive behavior in large trout, resulting in spectacular charges that are almost always visible. It works so well because it forces the fish to react to two basic instincts. First, it sees prey that has accidentally trespassed into its territory and now must escape. Second, the prey seems to be slightly injured and has some trouble swimming, but not to the extent that it can't escape.

Jerk-stripping is fast paced and covers lots of water. What you're trying to do is aggravate aggressive trout by covering every 3 to 4 feet of the river while working downstream by wading or drifting in a boat. It is not necessary to run multiple retrieves through the same area: if the fish sees the fly, it will generally respond on the first pass. The technique either creates the impulse to smash the fly quickly, or not at all. If a fish rolls at or swarms around the fly, you can make another cast, but solid hits do not usually follow a mock charge. It is, however, very difficult to convince yourself of this after seeing an assault.

While fishing with our good friend Jerry Dennis on the Manistee

River in the summer of 1995, we had a notable experience with mock charges. It was Jerry's turn at the oars, and Kelly was casting from the bow. They drifted into a large, deep bend that looked more like a spot for northern pike than for trout. Kelly continued to cast. On his third cast, a decent brown trout of about 19 inches followed his fly. The fish didn't connect, though, and by the time Kelly finished his retrieve and cast again they had floated 10 feet below the spot where the fish had showed. Kelly hauled a cast upstream into the same area and, much to his surprise, the fish charged again. And missed again. Now they were out of casting range, so Jerry pulled the boat to shore and both men waded back up to a reasonable position.

Thinking that the brown might be bored with the Zoo Cougar, Kelly switched to a Stacked Blonde and repeated his cast and jerk-strip retrieve. Again the trout charged the fly without a hookup. This continued through four more charges, and each time Kelly looked at Jerry like a wide-eyed schoolboy: "Did you see that? It did it again!" Jerry finally tired of this vaudeville show and waded downstream. Kelly decided to switch back to his original pattern, a size 2 Zoo Cougar, and give it one more try. After moving back into position, he cast again to the same spot. The fish showed *again* and actually hit the fly this time. Kelly "rolled" that trout, but was unable to set the hook. The fly was still in the water and had drifted at least 8 feet below the attack zone. Then, on its eighth try, it slammed the fly hard and hooked itself.

Kelly tried to affect an air of nonchalance and give the impression that he had planned all of this carnival behavior in specific sequence, but Jerry just rolled his eyes and climbed back into the boat. The fish was landed and released with high ceremony and loud benediction while Jerry sat muttering, "Kelly, your *luck* amazes me . . ." In his past several years of guiding and fishing more than 150 days each season, Kelly has seen only a half-dozen fish come to the fly more than once. But he still has faith it could happen again.

The jerk-strip presents your fly sideways to the fish, or perpendicular to the current. Understanding how your fly (the careless prey) would act in flowing water is vital. To escape, the prey will take the path of least resistance. Such a flight is downstream or across—not upstream, as a traditional retrieve would mimic. Knowing that prey will take the least-difficult course for a speedy retreat, you'll pull the fly directly back to your position, allowing the bow that forms in the line as a result of current drag to work to your advantage.

To maximize the effect of the jerk-strip retrieve, we use the fastest full-sinking lines available. Not sinking-tips. Full-sinkers. These are, by far, the most effective lines for keeping a streamer in the strike zone for the entire retrieve. Whenever we recommend full-sinking line to friends and clients, we hear the same response: "I don't like full-sinking lines because I can't mend them." Mending seems to be, in most anglers' minds, an overwhelming obstacle.

Generally, when you think about mending you think about reducing the line drag created by current. That's the beauty of the jerk-strip system, though: It uses drag as a positive. Drag forces the fly's head to turn downstream. The full-sinking line allows the fly to travel

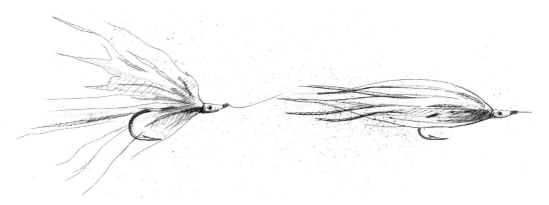

The fly on the left is in the fluttering, wounded posture during the pause of the jerk-strip retrieve. The fly on the right has resumed the flight profile.

through the same level in the water column throughout the entire retrieve, regardless of the depth you choose. A streamer does not have to be fished deep to be effective. With this retrieve we usually fish a streamer less than a foot under the surface. We are looking for the most aggressive fish and attempting to trigger a quick, instinctive reaction.

There is nothing dainty about this method. It is not an easy way to fish; it takes a fair amount of practice and strength to master. The cast is aggressive. The rate of retrieve is nothing less than feverish. The line control needs to be timed to perfection, but when it all comes together there is no more rewarding style of fishing for big trout.

The fly needs to smack the water *hard.* It has been said that this style of fishing is to dry fly-fishing what rock and roll is to the symphony. You cast the fly with force. This does not mean that you speed up your cast, but simply that you push all the way through your cast so the line energy does not run out before the end of your delivery. This is made much easier if you use a full-sinking line. The extra weight in the sinking line loads the rod quickly behind you so, given decent acceleration on the forward cast, even an intermediate caster can push a fly hard onto the surface with a great deal of accuracy.

Because you are not trying to fish the fly deeply, there is no reason to cast it upstream. Normally, you'll cast straight across the stream and attempt to keep the fly coming directly back to the boat. This is not a steadfast rule, however; there are times when you will have to cast directly upstream and/or directly downstream. You have no control over the way the river flows or how the structure is lying in the water, so you just have to present the fly from the best angle available. You should never pass on a spot because you cannot get the perfect cast. If nothing else, big fish are unpredictable. You can do many things to help turn the odds in your favor, but the bottom line is, the fish always make the rules. It's a time-tested theory: "You can't catch fish if your fly isn't in the water."

The initial impact on the water is the first thing the fish responds to. You are attempting to startle it and make it feel crowded or trespassed upon. This hard entry also serves notice to the fish that whatever it is that just hit the water could be injured. Try to think like the injured prey. Knowing there is something below you that would like nothing better than to make you into lunch gives a sense of urgency to the moment. (This also creates a subtle flow of adrenaline in the fisherman.) Once the fly is on the water, it is time to begin its "escape." Keeping your rod tip very close to the water (inches) and pointing at the fly, jerk the tip 12 to 20 inches downstream aggressively. At the end of the jerk quickly return the rod tip to its starting position and strip back the excess line. Be aware that the rod *tip* is moving the fly, so you will have to move your rod more than the 8 to 12 inches you want the fly to move, because the rod is going to flex and absorb some of the movement. You also have to deal with the current pushing your line. We have found that a rod movement of 12 to 20 inches moves the fly about 8 to 12 inches.

It is imperative to have good line control. Stripping back the line is not designed to move the fly, only to allow you to return the rod tip to its starting position so you can repeat the rod jerk. This needs to be done very quickly. You're trying to move the fly like a fleeing minnow, so repeat the jerk as fast as you can strip the excess line. We have found that the most productive method is to keep the fly moving at a pace that lets it pause just long enough for you to strip the line back to the starting position and then repeat the rod jerk. This gives the fly a momentary pause, which signals to the fish something could be wrong, and in turn triggers the instinct to kill the crippled prey. A pause of more than one second would tell your trophy trout that the prey has either died or is no longer a threat, so there is no need for it to attack or defend its territory.

This technique plays heavily on the fish's inability to shut off its basic predatory instincts of fight or flight, defend or die, and kill the weak to eat. Keep the fly moving: We are constantly amazed at how fast a big fish can appear and how little cover, if any, it takes to hide it. Continue your retrieve all the way back to the boat or, if you are wading, until the fly is within a few feet of your rod tip. But keep it moving.

An example of the importance of timing and movement occurred while Kelly was guiding on the Manistee River in northern Michigan in June 1996. It was unusually warm for June, almost 100 degrees F. The day was wearing on both Kelly and his client like wet shorts on a canoe seat. Dave was new to fly-fishing but had been fishing for 30 years with spinning gear. Since he was new at fly casting, Kelly spent most of the morning dodging fast-moving furred and feathered hooks. If they failed to hit Kelly they generally hit a tree. All in a day's work for a guide, but Kelly could see Dave's frustration mounting. When Dave's cast did hit the water, the fish were on the take, and he even managed to boat a few decent trout. The biggest problem Dave had was maintaining fly movement. He would usually smack the fly on the surface, then get in one rod jerk and maybe one strip; after that his timing would fail and the fly would lie motionless for two or three seconds. While this did fool the occasional village idiot, the big fish were not responding. Kelly and Dave finally decided to break for lunch around the next island and sit in the shade under a couple of the Manistee's big white cedars.

The river was low and clear. As they rounded the inside of the next corner the water narrowed to about 30 feet and the boat hung up on a sandbar. Kelly's 16-foot boat was almost sideways in the river. This was a 90-degree bend with numerous cedars hanging over the outside, and high tag alders on the inside.

As Kelly started to get out of the boat to push the boat off the sandbar, he noticed something: Joe Brooks seemed to have entered Dave's body, at least for one cast. Dave looked back at the tangled mass of tag alders, then looked forward through a hole in the cedars a scared grouse would have trouble flying through. Dave's—or Joe's (Kelly isn't sure who)—backcast went straight back through the tangles and then accelerated forward through the plate-sized opening with laser accuracy. The fly hit the water with a textbook *smack*. One rod jerk and a strip,

This magnificent 27-inch brown charged and ate a Stacked Blonde on wide open flat on a sunny mid-afternoon.

a second rod jerk and yet another strip. It was at this point that Joe must have found something else to do.

The biggest trout Kelly had ever seen come to a fly was charging forward with reckless abandon, his mouth open wide enough to swallow Cuba. When Dave saw that fish he let out a gasp that sounded like he had been shot. It was time for his third rod jerk, but nothing happened. Instead, both of his arms pushed forward at the fish and the fly went totally limp. Stunned, Kelly watched helplessly, stuck in his own momentary coma as 3 feet of brown trout slammed its mouth shut. The fish spun and created a hydraulic on the surface like that of a good back-stroke with a drift-boat oar. He was gone faster than a $20 bill in a casino. Dave stood shaking in the front of the boat, muttering a few things that the devil wouldn't repeat.

The lesson was learned the hard way, but learned nonetheless: "Keep the fly moving." Oh yes, Kelly did go back that evening, and the next morning, and the next two consecutive days thereafter in search of the trout with a mouth like a bass. Kelly guesses that brown is still waiting for Joe Brooks to show up again.

## The Line-Strip Method

The line-strip method is a more traditional way to create fly action and is highly effective under many conditions. It's especially valuable when rod movement is restricted. An example of this is fishing from the rear

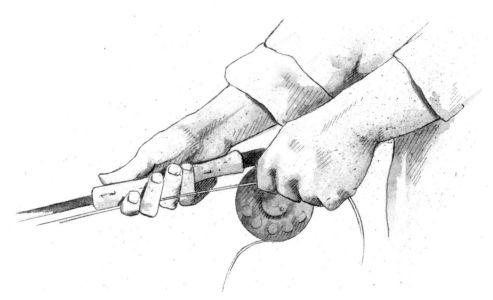

This illustration shows proper hand placement for stripping and striking. If the fly is in the water, the line should always be under the rod hand fingers. No exceptions.

of the boat to the right side. If you were to jerk-strip toward the rear of the boat, you would make your fly swim upstream. To strip to the left or downstream would quickly result in shortening your rod (hitting the boat). In this case, we find that a minimal loss of control is a small price to pay for moving the fly in the right direction—downstream. The same situation may occur in the tight quarters of a heavily wooded area along a small stream.

The line-strip method does require greater line-handling skill. The fly's action is totally dependent on your ability to strip in medium to long bursts (12 to 24 inches) very quickly without dropping your line. This is even more of a problem when you're fishing from a drifting boat. Most people have a tendency to strip only enough line to keep up with the boat, but not enough to move the fly.

It seems that this technique works best with flies that are weighted at the head, including coneheads and dumbbell/barbell head patterns like the Clouser series. The natural jigging action of a conehead fly creates a distinctive diving effect, and the line-strip greatly increases this specific action. The line-strip can also be very effective with a floating streamer. Allow the current to create a bow in your line (downstream) to start your fly heading downstream. Once the line has bowed, you can make the strips of varying lengths and beautifully mimic the motion of a fleeing prey. The bow also keeps a good amount of tension on the line, which helps you set the hook.

The line-strip method is essentially the same as the jerk-strip method in terms of the cast and the fly presentation. You must still load your rod aggressively on both your back- and forward casts. Push through the forward cast to accelerate and smack the fly onto the water's surface. When the fly hits the water, be ready to start stripping. This means you must make a clean, smooth transfer of the line from your line-holding hand to your rod hand. The line transfer will go under one or two of your forward rod-hand fingers. The rod should be close to the water—inches away. Holding the rod tip close to the water helps keep you from forming excess line with your rod swings. If the rod is kept too high and moves up and down while you strip, you will create small piles of slack line that you must strip in before you can move the fly. To strip line quickly, you must release pressure from your rod hand while stripping and then immediately reapply the pressure when you reach for the next section of line to be stripped. Reapplying the pressure between strips is where most problems occur. If the line is not secure between the cork and your finger when the fish strikes, the line will slide through your fingers as you raise the rod. You are left with an ugly situation. Either you backpedal to compensate (this becomes even uglier when fishing from a boat), or you execute a wild, out-of-control version of a salute as you helplessly scramble for the now flailing fly line. Net results are (1) Wet angler and no fish; (2) Dislocated shoulder and no fish; (3) Possibly both (1) and (2), and no fish.

After a couple of hours of this you might find a groove in your rod-hand fingers. This can be painful and will reduce your ability to grip line, but can be remedied in one of two ways. First, you can tape the grooved areas with a special tape created for this problem. Or second, you can fish a lot more and create a callus on your fingers like God intended.

## The Swing Method

It is our belief that when most people think of streamer fishing, the swing is what they envision. The old down-and-across method relies on fish that are looking for food. It is generally most productive for small to medium-sized trout. This is not to say that there have not been many large trout taken on the swing. Actually, we're sure that more large fish have been taken with this method than all the others combined, but not because anglers were deliberately seeking out big fish. More likely it is because this is the only system in wide use.

This technique can be very effective in some situations. Indeed, it is partially responsible for the design of the other styles of fishing that we have presented. It seems every time we heard a story about a big fish

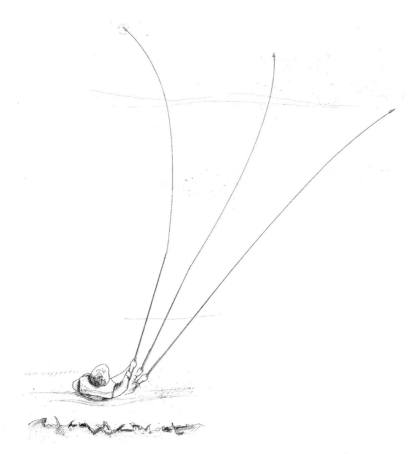

The down and across drift of the swing method is a great searching technique. Pay particularly close attention during the swing-out, or last part of the drift.

coming to a streamer, it went something like this: "Nothing was happening, so I put on a streamer and *bam,* the biggest fish I've ever seen." A classic swing-and-hope scenario. The angler had no expectation of catching a big fish; it was always a surprise. It was obvious to us that big fish ate streamers. We just wanted it to be less of a surprise and set out to see if we could make it happen on a more regular basis.

The swing method is a highly effective tool in the search for juve-

This beautiful coaster brook trout is from a small stream near Thunder Bay, Ontario. Bob caught several in just a few hours with Zoo Cougars and Butt Monkeys.

nile fish, fish that are still in feeding and holding stations, and the occasional larger fish. This method works best in shallow waters that hold trout looking for medium to small baitfish such as dace minnows. Generally associated with floating lines or short sinking-tips, the swing is a fun way to fish. It does not require the strength or line-handling skills required for the jerk-strip or the line-strip. The swing is best suited for small to midsized streamers—sizes 6 through 10. When working the swing, we like to use flies with lots of built-in action like marabous, feather wings, bunny-strip patterns of all sorts, and of course the Woolly Buggers and small Woolly Sculpins.

The swing method presents the fly noninvasively, so your delivery is similar to that you'd use for a dry-fly presentation. The fly is generally presented as a free-swimming minnow. It does not appear to be in a hurry or frightened. With the swing method, you cast across stream and allow the current to pull the fly down and across. Cast the fly as close to the shore or structure as possible. When it hits, allow the surface current enough time to create a small belly in your line. This tension on the line is what makes the fly swim and allows you to feel the strike. As your line swings downstream, the fly will follow, creating a large arc that straightens directly below you. After the swing is completed, step down and repeat. This way you cover a great deal of the river's surface area. You can greatly increase the system's effectiveness if you learn how to swim the fly by executing downstream mends of varying lengths; this gives you a great deal of control over the fly's course. By mending downstream, you can swing the fly fairly long distances parallel to the current flow. This allows you to swim the fly beside structures. If you choose to have the fly take a sudden turn toward you, simply lift your line up off the water by raising your rod tip. Try to lift the line off the water to make a wedgelike angle in it as close to the fly as possible. The fly will follow the line and change directions. You can also add short rod jerks and line-strips to create a multitude of actions in one presentation. Be careful not to overdo the rod jerks. You are trying to make the fly swim with short, smooth bursts. Because there

Bob hangs on to a large brookie that took a yellow Butt Monkey presented with the swing method. It hit just as the line straightened at the end of the swing.

is a bow in the line that creates tension, every movement of your rod tip will affect the fly. A short, 8-inch, upstream tip twitch will do everything you want. With practice, you can actually serpentine the fly in and out of structures without ever changing its action.

A combination retrieve with short rod jerks and line mends works exceptionally well for fishing topwater streamers of all sorts. Though it is not as effective as the jerk-strip for bringing up trophy fish, it is very fast paced and challenging when taken to its highest level. We prefer to use light flies that tend to float on their own, like Muddlers, small Woolly Sculpins, and pencil poppers. Yes, I said pencil poppers. They are great minnow imitations and they float like—well, like poppers.

The swing method is best suited to the wading angler. Using this

# Muddler Class

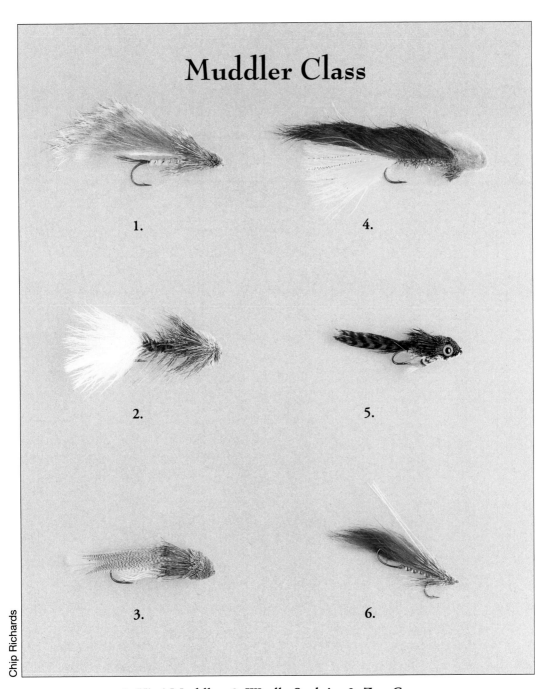

1.

2.

3.

4.

5.

6.

1. Kiwi Muddler  2. Woolly Sculpin  3. Zoo Cougar
4. Butt Monkey  5. Whitlock's Sculpin  6. Rattlesnake

# Baitfish Class

7. Zonker  8. Matuka  9. Stacked Blonde  10. Original Blonde  11. Gray Ghost
12. Glass Minnow  13. Big-Eyed Shiner  14. Tri-Color Bucktail

Chip Richards

# Crayfish and Leech Class

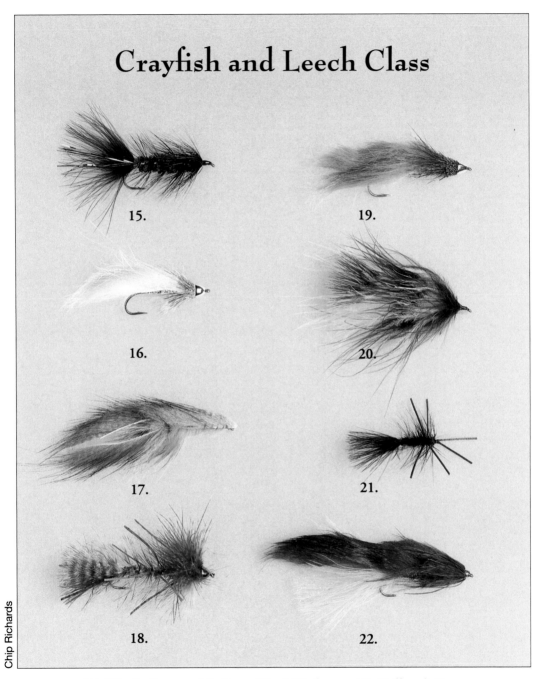

15. Woolly Bugger  16. Cone-Head Madonna  17. Galloup's Craw
18. Trick or Treat  19. Twin-Tail Madonna  20. Marabou Leech
21. War Bird  22. Strip Leech

# Attractor Class

23. Madonna  24. Mickey Finn  25. Cone-Head Marabou
26. Stacked Blonde (chartreuse)  27. Woolly Sculpin (chartreuse)
28. Rattlesnake (white and yellow)  29. Grau's Tiger  30. Silver Fox

system from a boat is difficult if the boat is moving. Because a boat usually moves at the same speed as the current, it's difficult to get the needed belly in the line to swing the fly.

As a general searching system it is hard to beat the swing, especially for exploring new water. When you are scouting water and not specifically hunting large fish, it can be a highly productive way to quickly determine if there are good numbers of resident trout around. The casting can be as graceful and delicate as a dry-fly presentation, satisfying the frequent need to be artistic. And the use of a streamer *always* presents the opportunity to raise the biggest trout in the river, and *this* satisfies the inextinguishable, deep-down desire to do battle with the largest fish in the ditch.

# Dredging

The "down-and-dirty" dredge is designed to fish a large fly at depth and very slowly. This technique searches for hungry trout that are resting close to the bottom. The dredge is not designed to make the fish move; instead it brings the meal to the fish. The dredge has proven itself as a great fish producer. The only problem is that the dredge is flat-out boring and slow. There is no real excitement until you are hooked up, and because you are fishing deep, you lose the visual impact of the chase and the strike. It is also somewhat problematic in heavily wooded areas. Such streams have a lot of natural or man-made deadfalls in the water, logjams. The fly rides on or near the bottom, resulting in a good number of snags and lost flies. Despite all this, there are days when nothing is happening and nothing is working, and it is then that you may want to pull the dredge out of the closet. It could save the day with a giant trout.

To effectively fish the dredge you need to remember that you are trying to present the fly as food. Not food that is trying to escape or invade—just food. One of the best dredge fishermen in the country, Tom Naumes, fishes a lot of white patterns. It is our belief that white or near-white may represent a dead or dying minnow that is losing its color. Bait fishermen have long been successful using dead, salted minnows for large trout, so it makes sense to follow suit in fly choice and delivery the way Tom has. It is logical and it is very effective.

To achieve a dead or dying effect with your fly, you will have to present it so that its head moves downstream, which means you have to mend your line downstream. Because of all this mending, most dredgers prefer sinking-tip lines to full-sinkers; they mend much more easily.

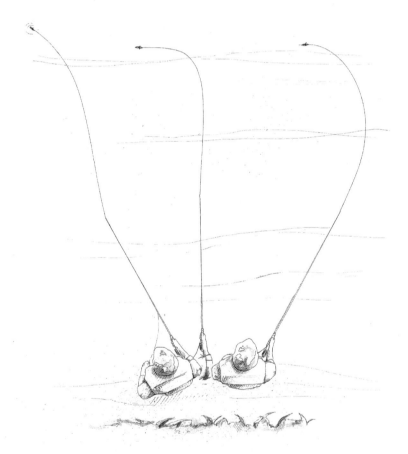

The dredge allows you to fish your fly very deep. Try to maintain a slow drift speed by feeding line as the fly passes below you.

To begin the dredge, aim your cast 45 degrees upstream. After the fly hits the water, pause, then throw an upstream mend in your line. This creates a wedge that pulls the fly downstream headfirst. Try to get as much of the sinking tip directly below the fly as soon as possible. As the tip sinks, execute an upstream mend. Try to get the sinking portion to sink unimpeded by floating line. Try to eliminate any bow in the line that would cause the sinking portion to be pulled from the bottom (this would speed up the swim rate of your fly). Try to achieve as close to a dead drift as possible. Once the line has passed downstream from your position, you will need to feed additional line into the drift, allowing the fly to sink farther. At the end of the drift, as the fly begins to swing out of the run, keep your rod low to the water and follow the arc of the swing with your rod tip. Try to make big, open swings with the fly. The larger the swing, the slower the fly will swim, and the slower it will begin its ascent.

You can also present the fly tail-first to the fish by reversing the mend sequence. Aim the fly up and across stream. As the fly hits the water, execute a large upstream mend. Try to keep the line above the fly at all times without pulling against the fly. As the fly swings past, follow the same sequence as before. Most people who have done a lot of dredging will tell you that a head-down presentation will far outfish one that's a tail-down.

## Tandem Flies

When anglers fish two flies together on the same cast, they're most often nymph-fishing and using a dropper rig. Less often, they use a dry fly as an indicator with a small nymph, or use two dry flies of different sizes, colors, or patterns to push the odds in their favor.

Rarely do you hear or read about fishing two streamers together, but it is an effective tactic that you should consider, particularly if you have trouble seeing your streamer clearly on the retrieve. Much of the excitement of streamer fishing is its visual aspects—the darting, swooning

This rainbow grabbed a chartreuse Woolly Sculpin. Yellow and chartreuse are highly visible to both angler and fish.

streamer fluttering its way back toward you, the openmouthed charge of an aggressive trout. If you cannot see the fly clearly, you cannot monitor its action and make adjustments in your retrieve as necessary. Just as important, you will probably miss the excitement of seeing the strike.

Greg Lilly, one of the premier guides in western Montana, reminded us of the advantages of fishing two flies at once. He explained that some people have difficulty seeing a dark fly on the retrieve. When this happens, many clients lose their concentration, pay less attention to moving the fly properly, and become much less effective at moving and hooking fish.

To counter this problem, Greg ties a large white or light-colored streamer to the leader, then adds a 2-foot dropper section to the bend of the first fly's hook to a smaller dark streamer. "Usually, a Woolly Bugger," he says. The big light-colored fly is easy to see and keeps your attention riveted to where it needs to be. If the fish want a light fly, you're ready. If they want a dark fly, it's available on the same cast.

Bob D'Ambruoso, an outfitter who specializes in wilderness float trips on Montana's Smith River, told us that he and his guides also employ this tactic with great success.

So we tested it in the Great Lakes basin. A size 2, yellow conehead Marabou Muddler followed by a size 8 Woolly Bugger did very well on the Au Sable; a light tan Zoo Cougar or cream Woolly Sculpin in front of a black or olive Madonna was incredibly effective on big Canadian brookies.

If you decide to try fishing tandem streamers, be sure to cast carefully and deliberately. Use stiff, abrasion-resistant tippet material between the two flies, and pinch down the barbs on the hooks.

## Fighting Fish

Quite possibly the most ridiculous phrase in fish-fighting lingo today is *confuse the fish*. This may have led more people down the path to lost trophies than any other cliché to date. This idea that erratic rod moments do something to confuse the fish reminds us of those hikers who wear bells in grizzly country. It is good for the hikers' peace of mind, but really only makes a noisy scat pile. After watching thousands of anglers, both novice and experienced, battle large fish, we can tell you who gets confused when an angler fights a trout without understanding how a fish reacts to pressure.

The second phrase that does a lot to confuse the angler (and not the fish) is *getting the fish off balance*. This one runs a close second to *confuse the fish*. A fish will not lose its balance due to anything other than fatigue or lactic acid buildup. And if either one happens you have probably played the fish far too long anyway; it'll stand a poor chance of survival after release. We'd like to help you understand and appreciate how a trout actually reacts to pressure, as well as what effects you the angler have and don't have.

To fully understand fish fighting, a few basic principles have to be understood. First, a fish has to follow its head. Second, a fish has no brakes. And third, fish do not have the power of conscious reasoning. They do not formulate plans of escape. They are simply surviving. As juveniles, their survival came from escaping into cover where an assailant could not pursue. It often serves as a bandage for our egos to believe that "that big trout really knew where it was heading"—that it must've done the same thing before in order to grow so large. The truth is, that trout was following a simple survival instinct. Using the flow of water to its advantage, a large fish depends on the same instincts to stay alive that it employed when it was a step or two down on the food chain.

Armed with the first two principles—"they follow their heads and have no brakes"—you should be able to outmaneuver most fish more times than not. Still, the most important factor you need to understand is the effect of water. Knowing how to use water—hydraulic pressure—to your advantage will greatly increase your fish-to-hand percentage.

Fighting fish is not unlike fighting of any style. Many of the basic rules of hand-to-hand combat require you to relax and to redirect your opponent's energy so that it works against him. Fighting fish is much the same. In order to redirect the fish's energy, you have to understand where the fish is and what effect the environment has on it. The fish is in a moving, pressuring environment that is almost always pushing against it. When you use the current to push the fish for you, half your problem is solved.

It is easiest to break this down into a limited set of variables. The trout has X number of moves it can make, and you therefore need only X number of responses.

To start with, break down the fish's alternatives. Is it upstream, across stream, or downstream? Is it heading upstream or downstream? That's five variables. Then there are at least 12 directions fish can move in—for example, head above level going away, head below level going away, and head below level coming at you. This gives you about 60 variables to deal with, not counting tree branches above the water and below, rocks, rapids, boats and the equipment within, fishing partners, tippet strength, hook strength, happy-handed netsmen, the fact that often you cannot see the fish clearly, and possibly your dog—otherwise it's virtually a shoe-in. These variables are why we say confusing the *fish* is not likely. Your superior brain capacity helps, unless you factor in the gray-matter depletion that happens to many of us immediately upon connection to a very large trout. Let's try this step by step.

First, you must determine what position the fish is in. Again, there are five possible positions for it:

1. Level in the current
2. In the current with its head facing up toward the surface
3. In the current with its head burrowing down

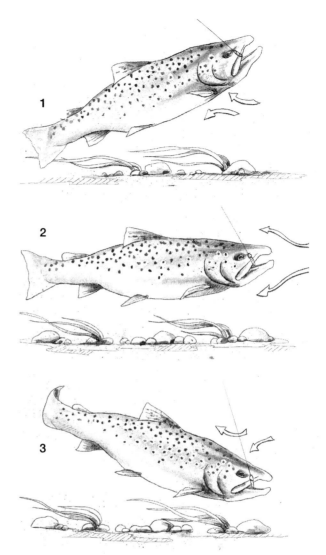

**1.** Advantage angler. Water and line pressure combine to force the fish's head up. **2.** This is a neutral position—a stand off. Attempt to gain control by lifting the fish's head. **3.** Advantage trout. The current is now working against the angler and the fish is in control. Use a low rod position to swing the fish and regain leverage.

4. Turning away from you and toward the other shore

5. Turning toward you, the angler

The fish is always making one or a combination of these moves. Understanding what you can do to help or hinder it is the key. If the fish is downstream from you, it's still doing one of these things; likewise a fish across or upstream. You need to understand what effect your moves and countermoves are having, if any, on it. And remember, the fish absolutely must follow its head, and it has no brakes.

You are first trying to do just one thing: to get the fish's head to come above level. When a trout's head angles above level, two good things happen. You gain leverage, a real advantage, and the moving water can now push the fish's body toward the surface. The fish has no brakes. It cannot stop, so it follows its head toward the surface. Now you are able to turn the fish back toward you. When its head begins to move in your direction, make a deliberate and smooth downstream, or toward-the-bank, pull with your rod. This will cause the fish to accelerate toward you, so be ready to take up a good deal of line. This is a critical point in the fight. The fish is accelerating and you are reeling. Now the fish will attempt to regain leverage by pushing its head downward, below level, so you must reposition your rod from the low, pulling position to a high, leveraging position. (*Key point: A high rod position* means the rod tip is high, not your hands. If at all possible, never let your hands get above chest level. When your hands go above your head you lose all control over the reel and your ability to bend the rod.) If the fish turns and regains its downward head position, it will have the upper hand again. This is especially true if its head has turned below level to a *burrowing* position. If you are still reeling when a fish in this position goes past you, it will most likely snap your tippet or pull the fly out, so be ready to give line. Repeat this procedure regardless of the fish's location. Lift and redirect. When the fish's head starts to move, you can confidently move your rod downstream, or away from the fish. The fish *must* follow, and you can take up line. When you have taken up all the line, you can repeat the process and take control of the contest.

But none of this will work unless you understand the hydraulics in and around the fish's location. Learning where the fish is lying relative to the current takes some time and observation. It does little or no good to try to make a rod pull downstream, or away from the fish, if it's already running away from you. It is imperative to have control of the fish's nose. And of course, there are times when you can do nothing but hold on. If the fish has turned away from you and is accelerating, you must wait until you feel there is a chance of gaining control over its head direction. If a fish turns away and down, you can often lead it around in a full circle with a low, slow rod sweep that follows the direction it was heading. But you have to be ready for that split second when you can gain control by lifting the rod. The fish may pause or turn; it might roll and seem to flounder or turn. The pressure will lighten slightly. You have to be ready and react quickly. This redirects the fish's energy and forces it to swim back at you. If you miss the split second of opportunity, you will watch helplessly as your trophy runs by.

During the past 20 years of guiding we have had many discussions on this topic with clients. One sunny mid-April day on the Pere Marquette River, Kelly was guiding a pair of relatively inexperienced steelhead fishermen. They had been hooking a fair number of fish, but their landing percentage was not impressive. At first, Kelly offered the standard old clichés to soothe the bewildered and fishless anglers: "We'll get the next one," and "Well, there wasn't much you could've done." Later, he gave more specific directives during the battles, and followed with "what you should have dones."

They stopped on an excellent run that held a large number of fresh steelhead, and decided to break for lunch to cool off and discuss a few of the subleties of fish control. Kelly had not been guiding this pair of men long, but he'd developed a pretty good relationship early on, and this allowed for frank discussions and plenty of good-hearted, constructive criticisms such as, "Galloup, you're full of it." After exchanging philosophies and "should'ves," one of the clients suggested that a demonstration was in order. Generally Kelly doesn't fish with or for his clients (mostly so they don't have the chance to say I told you so), but this time it seemed he had no choice. His cards had been called.

A good number of fish were in the river and they seemed eager to take. Kelly was fortunate to hook up quickly and even more fortunate to hook a relatively small fish of around 6 pounds. He admitted that everything did go right (more to his surprise than anyone else's); still, from start to finish, and including a complete move-by-move narrative, the fish was beached in less than 1 minute, 40 seconds. That steelhead followed the script of Kelly's earlier discussions on fighting fish precisely, right down to the split-second pause that allowed Kelly to quickly end the contest. He had the anglers' attention for the rest of the day and no more arguments about his "you should'ves." No, Kelly never did tell them that the fish was pretty much a gift from God and possibly a paid insider from the guides' association. He simply rowed down the river bigger than John Wayne basking in at least two minutes of fame and glory.

~

This leads to that other fish-fighting cliché, *getting the fish off balance.* You've no doubt seen people making erratic rod-angle changes during the fight. The fish makes a run of some distance, and the angler takes the rod hard right and then hard left, possibly several times. The thought here is to confuse the fish or get it "off balance." Right. This tactic is detrimental in all categories! All it does, besides confuse *you,* is help loosen the hook in the fish's mouth. If the fly is 30 feet or more from you and you start fanning your rod back and forth, you have little effect on the fish or fly. Worse, you make the fly rock back and forth in the fish's mouth, helping to open a bigger hole. And in the process you may have missed a subtle move by the fish—a telltale sign that might have gained you a momentary advantage.

Prove it to yourself. Go into your yard with a friend and have him pull 30 or 40 feet off the reel. Hold the end of the fly. We hope we don't have to tell you to be careful and to use a hook that has been debarbed. Have your companion fan the rod back and forth and see what effect this has on your fingers. You will quickly note that there is *no* significant change in the fly or pressure and you, like the fish, will *not* become confused or off balance.

Jumping fish present another set of problems with their own set of solutions. For a jumping fish, the old *bow to the king* rule almost always works. What's "bowing to the king"? It's when a fish jumps and you point and lower your rod tip to meet it. This term comes from Atlantic salmon fishing, Atlantics being the "king of all fly-rod fish." By lowering the rod tip you are attempting to give the fish enough slack that it does not land on a tight leader and break it. Still, too much of a good thing can be bad. Lowering the rod is fine, but a radical response—a huge lunge forward—is not. This gives the fish too much free line. When it hits the water again, it's not just going to sit there. It's going to see if it's free. If you've got 3 or 4 feet of slack, the fish can regain momentum and the upper hand.

We suggest instead a moderate dip to the fish. By this we mean you should *push* your rod at the fish, and do so just enough to give slack line. Don't push so much that you create 3 feet of excess line on the water, or throw yourself out of position. At the split second the fish hits the water, you can once again strive for control of its head.

Which brings us to another scenario: the fish out of water. This situation results in the loss of more big fish than any other we know of. The point when a large fish is close to being whipped and flounders just below you is critical in the contest. A large trout's head often comes out of the water for that last little roll. We call this "gator rolling." The fish is close. We think we've won. Its head breaks the water surface and makes two or three rolls like a gator. With its mouth wide open, this rolling results in a pulled-out fly.

When a fish's head comes out of the water you lose the hydraulic cushion you had under water. The net result isn't much different than hanging the fish off the side of the boat 2 feet above water: The hook comes free, the fish is lost. To properly combat this, when you see the fish's head come to the surface, take your rod low and to the side. This keeps the fish's head in or close to the water, and the side pressure stops it from being able to roll.

## Angler Position and Movement

Like any good fighter you have to move. All the rod moves in the world can't make up for bad angler position. If at all possible, never let a fish get too far below you. This may mean chasing the fish, but you lose almost all control if a trophy-sized fish gets more than 30 feet below you in the current. At 30-plus feet you have little control; all the fish has to do is hang below you like a dog on a leash. Aside from the discomfort of the hook it's feeling little resistance, and often it can stabilize itself and regain its strength. In our (collective) 40-some years of guiding, this is the number one cause of the big-fish losses we've witnessed. You can sometimes manhandle smaller trout back up to you, but any self-respecting carnivore-sized brown, brookie, cutt, or rainbow will eat you up, spit you out, and leave you standing like the empty trailer by the side of the road.

# Landing, Handling, Releasing, and Photographing

Everything is right with the world and you are about the land the biggest trout of your life. The monster is 3 feet from your legs and you have to make a decision: "Do I do what I tell everyone else to do and let this fish go, or do I try to 'back-door' him to the closest taxidermist I can find?" We hope you decide on the former, realizing that this trout is what has been keeping you fly-fishing all these years. Whatever you decide, though, you had better land the fish first.

Jac Ford

Here is a combination of *good* things: a large fish supported gently, a non-abrasive netbag, and a nice photograph from an interesting angle.

It is our belief that a good net saves the lives of a lot of fish. Fish that you intend to set free may end up just as dead as the one on the wall above the fireplace through careless handling. Poor handling of fish results in death, and that's a stone-cold fact. A net allows you to end the fight sooner than does trying to hand-land or beach the fish. The net also allows you to keep the fish in the water while preparing for the traditional ceremony of photographing the beast. If you decide to hand-land the fish, remember *not* to grab it near the throat, or to squeeze it in order to stop it from escaping. If any portion of that is vague, then a net is in order. We have watched countless anglers (including ourselves) wrestle with fish for a ridiculous period of time when they could have been netted with little or no bother.

Of course, as longtime steelhead and salmon guides, we have also seen more than our share of botched net attempts. On any given night at the watering hole where guides meet to talk over their day, you can be assured that this topic is the one drawing the most laughter. It seems that netting is somewhat of an afterthought for anglers. Which is strange, because it's at the net that many fish are lost.

This is a good time to point out that the fish we hope you will be catching require a bigger-than-average trout net. When you shop for a net, make sure the bag will hold a trophy fish. All your technique and practice will be for naught if the fish will not fit in the net. We suggest a soft cloth or linen bag for nets. Such nets are less likely to remove the fish's natural mucus layer or cause abrasions to its skin. Cheap, usually aluminum-framed nets come with abrasive, hard-nylon net bags that scrape the fish's skin. Avoid these. Spend a few extra dollars and buy a net with a width (across the bow) of at least 16 inches and a length opening (from the base of the handle to the tip of the bow) of 18 inches. A long handle is helpful—20 to 24 inches is just fine. These higher-grade products are very sturdy and most often come with cotton bags deep enough to hold large fish.

To properly net fish you need to remember one thing: *Net the head.* With a small fish you can scoop, because the net will totally surround it. But big trout require a plan.

Make sure you are in a spot where you can move without stumbling. Try to get out from under any trees that might stop you from being able to lift your rod tip high enough to bring the fish's head to the net. Then *net the fish's head.* If you try to net it from the tail, it'll feel the net and run from it. As you lead the fish to the net, have your line tight and raise the rod tip to the point that the fish's head is on the surface. Then make a push with the net under its head, and keep pushing right through the fish. If it feels the net it will still lunge forward, but it will be swimming *into* the net. As you go for the push, give yourself some slack in the line just as the net starts to go under the fish; otherwise, you will knock the fly out or break the line.

When a fish is lost at the net it's generally because the angler made a swipe at its side or tail, or didn't have the confidence to make a deliberate move. If you are fishing with a partner, make sure *you* say when the fish should be netted. Don't allow wild swipes at your fish. This panics both fish and fisherman. Make sure you have control. When you feel you can direct the fish's head at the netsman, tell your friend to net the fish. Again, when he pushes the net you have to give slack or you will break the line. It's a tricky balance, but critical.

If you are attempting to beach or tail a large trout, it is even more important to have complete control. The same set of rules applies as when you're netting. You have to find a spot that will allow you to get on the shore, along with the fish, with enough room to maneuver your rod and direct the fish's head to shore. Again, this means no obstructions on the shore side. Attempt to get downstream from the fish. Apply enough tension on the line to raise its head into the surface film. When its eyes are out of the water you have achieved the perfect situation. Use a smooth and steady pull of the rod to direct the fish toward shore. When it feels bottom, it will try to swim away. If you're applying the right amount of pressure—just enough to keep its head up and pointing to shore—the fish's attempt to escape will force it onto the beach.

When you're tailing a fish, you have to be absolutely sure it's tired enough to get close enough to you without spooking. This is the main reason we don't recommend tailing. Fish this tired are often hard to revive. If you are confident that you can tire and control the fish without exhausting it, grab and firmly grip the trout at the wrist (just forward of the tail) with a cotton or fleece glove. The glove allows you to hold the fish without squeezing too hard. A wet glove grips the fish without removing his protective slime and holds his tail as though it were dry. Fleece gloves also work well, but make sure they don't have some sort of leather or rubber surface. Such a surface is fine for gripping your rod handle, but it's not much better for holding on to a fish than your bare hands.

After you've landed your fish you will likely want to pick it up and hold it momentarily. If you do this, remember that a fish lives in a cushion of water. When you lift it out of water it no longer has that support. We suggest you keep the fish very close to the net, lifting it only slightly out of the water. If at all possible, keep its belly in the water. If you are going to lift the fish up for a photograph—and we all do—support it near its head (without squeezing) and by the wrist in front of its tail. We keep cotton gloves in the boat for just this purpose. Make sure the person taking the picture has set up ahead of time so you are not lifting the fish up and down needlessly. We like to take photographs as soon as possible after netting the fish and *before* it has been revived. Fish are easier to handle at this time, and you don't have to interrupt the resuscitation process. Never keep the fish out of the water for more than 10 seconds.

Shy of going into f-stops and aperture settings, we thought we would share a few things that have helped us photograph clients and each other with trophy fish over the years. If you're the one with the camera, make sure the sun is at your back or quartering to your back. If it's directly at your back, watch out for shadows on your subject. Lose your sunglasses, and if at all possible take off your subject's sunglasses, too. Now you can see the joyful expression in the eyes. A dash of color always helps a picture—a red hat, a red bandanna, anything to give a little kick to the drab colors we anglers usually wear. Keep your subject's head in the shot. Many lousy photos of great moments are due to a headless angler. Don't be afraid to include some scenery in a few shots. And shoot some tight close-ups of the fish. If you carry a single-lens reflex camera, be sure to attach a polarizing filter to cut glare. The polarizer will allow you to shoot some crisp photographs of your trophy under water. These shots, if composed properly, are beautiful and dramatic.

That adrenaline rush that's pumping through your veins can sometimes cloud your reasoning. We see this quite often when a big fish is in the net. Keep a careful eye on your fishing partner and remind her to admire the trophy while in the water so it can continue to breathe.

We know a western guide who sports an "18-inch" tattoo on his arm. He stated, in Kelly's presence, that the distance from the tip of his index finger to the tattoo near his elbow was *exactly* 18 inches. When Kelly and another guide held him down and checked the accuracy with a tape measure, they found it to be 17 inches. Guides will go a long way to make a client happy, including plunging a bare arm into cold water next to a submerged fish, and fudging an extra inch!

This is what it's about. Being in a beautiful spot, catching a big fish, photographing the monster, and then releasing it: There is no better feeling in the angling world. With a good photograph and a fond memory you have it all. If you feel the need to have a more tangible memento in the form of a mount, there are many skilled taxidermists who specialize in synthetic reproductions. As a taxidermist for over 15 years, Kelly has come to the conclusion that properly done, synthetic mounts are superior in every way. Remember to get very accurate measurements—both length and girth—as well as good close-up color photographs of your fish. Such close-ups should include one shot of just the head, one of the body for

Cradle the fish in the water. Try to keep your trophy relaxed, and only lift the head from the water for a brief, photographic moment.

spot patterns, and one of the entire fish. Note any peculiarities of the fish, and photograph them if you want them to show up on the reproduction. We hope you will agree with us that trophy fish play a vital part in the well-being of river systems and are far too valuable to catch only once.

## Releasing Large Trout

When releasing a fish that has been played for a long time, we like to let it rest near structure where it can hide its head under something like a log. Make sure there is reasonable water depth. We often will put fish under the boat when it is in 2 feet or less of water. The fish will often stay right where you place it for a long period. If it has not moved on its own after 10 minutes or so, we usually flush it out or simply move the boat. Either gets the fish active enough to swim to another resting spot. If the fish does not seem to have its strength back after a few minutes, we hold and move the fish into the current to assist it further. We are not sure if any of this helps, but it can't hurt, and a fish in the boat has 100 percent chance of death.

∾

All the techniques presented in this chapter are based on the same premise: Big fish are predators, masters of their domain. They fear

This beautiful, 27-inch male brown from the lower Au Sable is being carefully revived in a gentle side current. A polarizing filter was used to cut the surface glare.

nothing and take whatever they want. As alpha predators, they behave as do all dominant predators—from the mighty grizzly to the voracious dragonfly. Kill or be killed and defend what is yours. All predators live by the same set of instincts. Most important is territory. If a trout cannot defend its territory, it cannot eat, and if it can't eat, it dies. Predators are specifically designed to kill the weak and the injured. Understand these character traits of a dominant, trophy trout, and you can tap into its dark side and make it respond. Remember, an instinctive reaction cannot be shut off the way hunger can. If you're not hungry, you don't have to eat, but if you're startled, you have to jump. It's instinct.

# chapter five

# Today's Most Effective Patterns

M any factors contribute to the continued effectiveness—the re-peated, overall seductive power—of a streamer pattern. Better hooks and new materials are part of the equation, but only a part. Classic streamers like the Gray Ghost, the Blonde series, and the original Muddler enjoy uniform, durable popularity due to one critical element: They were thoughtfully designed. The Gray Ghost, when wet, slims down into a graceful silhouette; its carefully selected colors and jungle cock eye marry and blend. The net effect is a grand illusion of wandering prey.

Joe Brooks wanted a fly that represented a substantial meal, that moved water, and that was relatively easy to cast. He took the Blonde series—originally designed by Homer Rhode Jr. to achieve all this in salt water—and adapted it slightly for use on large trout in the smooth tailouts of pools and heavy runs in the rivers of Tierra del Fuego and Montana. Blondes work as well today as they did in the 1950s. And Don Gapen's creation, the Muddler, is the ultimate testament to conceptualization and innovative design. The mighty Nipigon is paved with sculpins, and its magnificent brook trout reach the size of respectable salmon because of this abundance. The Muddler's clipped, rough deer hair head and slim, tapered profile came only after a careful, studied analysis. That this fly, roughly unchanged, endures today as a highly successful imitation is a tribute to its original design. The fact that the Muddler has inspired an entire class of streamer patterns is the ultimate acknowledgment of Gapen's achievement.

∾

Pattern design in a pure form comes from conceptualization, thinking about what you want that fly to accomplish and represent. Then, through an understanding of materials and the way they respond when properly applied to a hook, the desired effect is created.

As an example of the process, let's look at Kelly's now popular Zoo

In this top view of a swimming Zoo Cougar note the tapered shape that closely approximates that of a live sculpin.

Here are top and bottom views of large sculpins centered around the bottom view of a Zoo Cougar.

Cougar. This fly's final form did not appear overnight. It was designed in steps. First, Kelly wanted the fly to be *broadly* representative of the sculpin family throughout North America. Second, he intended to fish the pattern at 2 feet (or less) of depth in the water column. Third, and perhaps most important, he wanted it to "catch" the current and flutter when not being stripped.

The Zoo Cougar's broad, flat, clipped head (deer hair) and flank feather wing provide it with the necessary profile. The fact that the fly is unweighted means that the depth at which it swims is controlled by the density of the sinking line and the speed of the retrieve. The wide head and flat wing catch and hold moving water, causing the fly to dart, weave, and *swoon* on pauses in the retrieve; the marabou tail flutters enticingly. The end result is a fly that is a terror; large trout, steelhead, smallmouth, and northern pike absolutely smash it.

During its first two years of field-testing we used the Cougar with great success on coaster brook trout in the Nipigon drainage. Close friend and guide Scott Smith named the pattern: "It's kind of fat like a zoo cougar, but when it's wet and swimming it slims down like a cougar in the wild."

The fly's success with truly large trout caused its fame to spread quickly, and Kelly was often asked if he had tried using a ram's wool head. The answer was yes, he had considered it, but no, he hadn't tried it. A wool head would certainly absorb water and cause the fly to swim deeper, but that was not what the fly was designed to do. It was designed to trigger a response from aggressive fish in shallow water. The fact that the pattern also works well when fished deeper than 2 feet is an added bonus, but adding a wool head is not designing a new fly.

Everyone dreams of creating a great new pattern, perhaps the next Muddler or Woolly Bugger. We encourage you to experiment—to analyze a problem or opportunity, conceptualize a solution, design, test, and finalize. But remember that adding a few strands of Krystal Flash or changing a color does not make a new pattern, and it doesn't mean you can change the name to Bob's Circus Cougar. That "new" fly of yours is still just a Zoo Cougar.

In today's high-tech society there are more material choices available to fly-tyers than could've been imagined even a few years ago. Still, the great, classic streamers have changed very little, if at all. A few float longer, some glitter and flash a bit more, but few have really changed. The evolution or development of truly new flies is born of the need for something more effective. Look, for instance, at the exploding or floating nymph with its dubbing ball wing, and the trailing shuck emerger with its Antron tail. These are simple changes at first glance, but they represent a step forward in concept and design. And it is rarely a loose-handed, casual tyer who creates an effective and lasting pattern.

Many of the most dramatic new designs, including the creative application of new synthetic materials, came from the saltwater ranks. The newest saltwater patterns combine lifelike shape and motion with durability, flash, and appropriate color. Flies like the ALF Baitfish, Bronze

Mullet, Peterson's Baby Bunker, and Whit's Deep Baitfish come immediately to mind as examples of superb design. With modifications in color and size, their basic designs serve as a good foundation for adaptations to freshwater species. We always look at the new saltwater patterns first when a new fly-fishing catalog arrives.

There are many excellent books on fly-tying materials currently in print. These, and the angling magazines, have a wealth of information on furs, hairs, feathers, synthetics, and hooks, and we will not attempt to replicate that information here. It is all easy to access either on the printed page or through the Internet. Suffice it to say that when you're tying, it's crucial to know what effect a material choice will have on the action of your fly. Tie a prototype and test it in the water. A sculpin pattern that looks terrific in the vise may spin like a top when retrieved through current, because you glued the bottom hairs on a spun deer hair head.

## The Sculpin or Muddler Group

Let's go back to Don Gapen on the banks of the Nipigon. After scratching his head he began to conceptualize the solution to a problem. Soon enough thereafter he had tied his revolutionary prototype Muddler, with its clipped deer hair head, and began to knock the fins off huge brookies. As they say on Broadway, a star was born.

This fly has been and continues to be so successful worldwide that *any* fly with a wide, flat head (particularly one spun from deer hair) is often referred to as a Muddler. This is, of course, inaccurate, but it does testify to the universal admiration for the pattern—and we won't go against this tradition. We will put any fly that has a wide, flat head, be it wool, deer hair, or other, and is generally representative of sculpins in our Muddler group.

In many trout rivers in North America, in fact throughout the world, sculpins are common baitfish. Therefore patterns that effectively represent sculpins have great importance. Gapen's pattern—with its

These sculpins are on either side of a dark Woolly Sculpin pattern. A Woolly Sculpin, properly tied, presents realistic views from top, bottom, and side perspectives.

wide, flat, and rough head, its tapered profile, and its slim rear end—set the engineering design standard for sculpin imitations. Still, many anglers, ourselves included, found over the years that when tied in sizes equivalent to the natural creature, the Muddler did not duplicate the sculpin as closely as we wanted. Big trout are pickier now that we are on the edge of the millennium. Something new had to be designed.

Four elements are absolutely critical to an effective sculpin or Muddler—shape, size, action, and color. Shape is vital because of the unique silhouette displayed by the natural. Size is important for technically accurate representation and, more importantly, because big trout seem to prefer a certain size of sculpin. They appear to seek out adults, and in most rivers adults range from 2½ to 3¾ inches long. This observation comes from actual autopsies of more than 300 trophy trout (20 inches or larger) over the past years. (Kelly owns a taxidermy business, and although he encourages synthetic reproduction mounts, he does take the opportunity to examine the stomach contents of all large trout delivered to his shop.) Action is important to all streamers. If you don't know how a prey item moves and acts within its environment, you cannot dress a suitable impostor. Certain materials create lift (deer hair), while others create drop (ram's wool). Applying materials with different characteristics provides a wide range of possible movement based on retrieve rates. It is even possible to create a fly that will bounce up and down like a lead-head jig if you so desire. Finally, we know that color is an important factor in sculpin imitations—in all flies, for that matter. Yet it seems to be the single most volatile factor in achieving success from day to day. Yellow is probably the most consistent producer over an extended period, but this can change quickly—very quickly. Given today's catch-and-release ethic, a fish that has been stung frequently by yellow Rattlesnakes will learn to avoid them. At least for a while.

Attention to seemingly minute details is important. Even with a great design, a fly that's seen a minor flaw in assembly often fails to produce. As an example, we recently field-tested a few immaculately tied popular sculpin patterns. These were taken right off the shelf at the Troutsman fly shop in Traverse City. Tied by a large and reputable commercial firm, these flies all looked absolutely perfect. Filled with anticipation, we began pitching the masterpieces to the currents.

But the fly would spin whenever he tried to impart any action. It would flip upside-down and roll over, playing havoc with his leader. We changed flies several times but each one from that batch acted exactly the same. Finally we sat down and examined the flies closely. This particular batch featured sharp edges on the bottom of the head as well as glue applied to the underside of the head. This created a clean-looking and very durable fly, but also one nearly impossible to sink. The sharp underside edges acted like rudders and would flip the fly over when stripped. However, when we simply let the fly swing in the current with no imparted action—almost a straight-downstream dredge—the pattern stayed upright and looked great.

This is an example of a production run of flies that were tied for durability and looks to the detriment of function. They looked fantastic and would last forever, but would they perform as they should? No. The problem is easily corrected by softening the edges and not gluing the bottom of the head. This alleviates the rudder effect and allows water to saturate the fly evenly, keeping the top and bottom of its head at a constant density. Attention to detail is the key to success.

The following list presents the modern sculpin imitations, or Muddlers, that we feel are most effective for trophy trout:

1. Kiwi Muddler
2. Woolly Sculpin
3. Zoo Cougar
4. Butt Monkey
5. Whitlock's Sculpin
6. Rattlesnake

Each of these flies has at least one unique, tantalizing feature that is the product of conceptualization and careful design. The color photographs and recipes in this chapter will, we hope, clearly illustrate each pattern's attributes. As a brief overview we suggest that the Kiwi Muddler's rabbit-strip wing, attached behind the head only, combines durability with undulating, lifelike action; the Woolly Sculpin combines Woolly Bugger action with the rough profile and proportions of an adult sculpin; the Zoo Cougar's flat overwing cups and grabs the current, causing the fly to flutter and appear disabled; the Butt Monkey combines the action of a fur wing with a sinking head of ram's wool; a Whitlock's Sculpin presents an accurate profile with a realistic blend of color; and the Rattlesnake's devious design stings and holds fish that strike "short" or directly down on the head of the fly.

We assure you that all of these patterns have been rigorously field-tested over time. Jac Ford, a good friend who guides in Montana and Michigan, took a dozen prototype Zoo Cougars with him on a trip west a few years ago. He explained that his supply quickly disappeared—the big fish in the Yellowstone and Beaverhead "took them and kept them."

The next year more than 100 Zoo Cougars went west with Jac.

## Baitfish—The Original Streamer Class

There has always been some measure of debate over the proper defini-
tion of the word *streamer*. Is it strictly a minnow imitation? Is it strictly
a minnow imitation tied with a feather wing? The classic understanding
is that flies tied with a feather wing to represent baitfish are called
*streamers,* while those tied with hair wings, either natural or synthetic,
to produce the appropriate profile are called *bucktails.* And of course
there is overlap. Many patterns use both hair and feathers to achieve the
desired result. For our purposes we will refer to flies that are designed
to imitate baitfish other than sculpins, regardless of whether they use
feathers, hair, or a combination, as streamers.

The baitfish class is wide and varied. It provides endless opportunity for new fly design and, to date, has sponsored the widest range and
number of streamer patterns. This makes perfect sense when you consider the sheer number of small, prey-sized fish that can be in a given
stream at any point in time. Dace, chubs, darters, juvenile trout, and
shiners all share the same currents and depths contending for food and
safety. Before the Woolly Bugger and leech craze began, you would be
hard pressed to find (besides a Muddler or two) much other than baitfish patterns—classic streamers and bucktails—in most fly wallets,
stores, or books.

The most dramatic changes in baitfish-class flies during the past
decade are due to the proliferation of synthetic materials. Artificial hair
with increased sheen and durability in vibrant, new colors; plastic eyes
of various hues, shapes, and weights; Mylar body material; epoxy coatings—the list not only goes on, but grows each year. And tyers have
taken full advantage of the new materials to push fly design dramatically. As we've noted, a high percentage of the more stunning developments have originated with saltwater tyers. As a group, trout anglers
seem less likely to embrace new synthetics like plastic hair and epoxy.

They tend to favor the more traditional bucktail, hackle wing, and marabou. Still, synthetics are merging with the traditional trout-fly materials and the blends result in some incredible patterns.

The key elements of a great baitfish imitation may sound familiar; they are silhouette, action, size, and color. And of these, silhouette is the most critical. Achieving a proper underwater profile is the biggest problem tyers face in designing and constructing a good streamer. The most prominent example of this dilemma is presented by marabou streamers. While in the vise, a marabou streamer may be an inch high and quite thick, but when stripped through the water this bulk will slim and compress dramatically. The "wet" result as viewed by a trout may be only ⅜ inch high and less than ¼ inch wide. This is definitely something to consider when designing baitfish imitations.

Many of the newer streamers, particularly those inspired by saltwater patterns, solve the compression or reduction problem by combining traditional with space-age materials that do not collapse onto themselves when wet. Overall wet appearance—size and profile—is the issue, not action. Action is generally not a significant concern with either traditional natural materials or modern synthetics, because design dictates that the material be fastened to the hook (usually near the head of the fly) so that it flows freely with the current. This is especially true with marabou—the one material that, as yet, no synthetic has been able to duplicate. Fur strips, especially rabbit and mink, rank a close second to marabou for lifelike action. Although we encourage the use of synthetics for shine, bulk, and durability, we still believe that nothing approximates the shimmering, lifelike qualities of marabou and bunny strips.

Color is a major factor in most baitfish patterns, and the blending of color is critical when you're attempting to represent a specific kind of baitfish. Most of these small creatures sport a distinct stripe or demarcation line between two colors. The blacknose dace is an obvious example, but almost all minnows have a two-tone appearance. This is obviously important in designing and tying properly representative streamers.

Although it's not yet understood how color motivates a trout, some very similar responses are generated by like colors from pattern type to pattern type. This similarity in response is best illustrated by sculpin and baitfish patterns in two colors—yellow and chartreuse.

Neither of us has ever seen any living thing under water that was chartreuse in color; neither have we seen much in bright yellow. Yet these are two very productive colors for both sculpin and baitfish patterns; we simply would not be on the water without them. And their production is not limited to what you might think of as obvious conditions—dark sky and high, dirty water. Sometimes they will rack up an impressive score under bright skies and in clear, low water. When big trout are "on" yellow and chartreuse, it doesn't seem to matter whether we fish a leech, a Muddler class, or a Blonde. The fish are excited more by the color than by the pattern.

Following are our favorite patterns for this class of prey. Most are modern designs, but two classics appear. We simply have not been able to improve on the perfection of the Gray Ghost, and the original Blonde still performs very nicely.

7. Zonker
8. Matuka
9. Stacked Blonde
10. Original Blonde
11. Gray Ghost
12. Glass Minnow
13. Doc's Big-Eyed Shiner
14. Tri-Color Bucktail

We like Zonkers in a wide variety of wing colors, including black, olive, dark brown, natural, white, yellow, and chartreuse. In our experience the best body colors are gold and pearl. Matukas can be tied in any combination of colors, but seem to work best in "natural" blends that present the two-toned, striped effect we referred to earlier. Our Blonde and Stacked Blonde colors of choice are white, yellow, and chartreuse. These flies should be tied very large on heavy hooks of 4X long, size 2 or larger. The Gray Ghost is not to be taken lightly or thought of as a regional fly for the Northeast. Carry some in sizes from 10 to 2.

Both the Glass Minnow and the Big-Eyed Shiner evolved from saltwater patterns. Dave Ellis developed both after careful scrutiny of several modern saltwater sardine and glass minnow imitations. They are extremely effective on both brown and rainbow trout.

## Leeches and Crayfish

Throughout Kelly's run as a premier taxidermist, the prey item he's found second most often in the stomachs of trophy trout is the crayfish (the sculpin is first). The point spread between first and second is slim. Vegas gamblers would have a hard time setting odds on which food source is consumed more frequently based on abundance. It is not unusual to find partially digested remnants of both in the stomach of a large trout; frankly, this is the case more often than not.

In terms of autopsied evidence, leeches contrast starkly to sculpins and crayfish. The general group of leech and lamprey (and worm!) prey items is one of the groups most widely imitated by fly tyers, yet Kelly has *never* found a leech in a trout's stomach. And our local rivers support them, as well as significant populations of chestnut lampreys that range from 2 to 12 inches in length. It is not unusual to find one or more *on* a trout, but never have we seen one *in* a fish! Still, this should in no way discourage you from using leech and lamprey patterns. We have seldom found a worm or night crawler either, but everyone knows how trout like to eat them.

In our estimation, the flies in the leech group (specifically the Woolly Bugger) have had more impact on streamer fishing than those in any other class. If there is one fly that could be almost guaranteed to be in every angler's box worldwide, it would be the Woolly Bugger. Not since the Muddler Minnow roared onto the scene in the 1950s has any one pattern enjoyed such immediate, universal acceptance.

Originally tied leechlike in dark colors—black tail and hackle and dark olive body; all dark brown; all black—this fly has seen more stylistic adaptations and color changes than Dennis Rodman's hair. This is the go-to pattern for most fly-anglers. It is tied in sizes from 18 to 3/0, in colors from black to neon chartreuse. It tempts nearly all fish, from beaver pond brookies to barracudas and tarpon. The Woolly Bugger has probably accounted for more big fish of all kinds in the past 15 years than any other fly. Two major reasons for this are that it is almost impossible to fish incorrectly—nearly idiot-proof—and it is incredibly easy to tie.

The Woolly Bugger has always been considered a leech pattern, at least primarily. But we think it is probably ingested occasionally as a stonefly nymph. And in the right colors, it makes a very good, suggestive crayfish pattern.

Crayfish have been "discovered," so to speak, as a preferred source of protein for trophy trout, and subsequently many new patterns have recently come to light. More and more fly anglers are learning to use crayfish flies effectively; they're now among the most effective and consistent producers.

After watching crayfish for many hours, and poking scores of the little crustaceans to make them swim, we have arrived at some conclusions. Not the least of which is that the standard Woolly Bugger is a pretty representative copy and a darned good pattern. When you watch crayfish swim (as opposed to crawl), the most significant feature you notice is that the claws come together and trail behind the scooting crayfish's body—much like the marabou tail on a Woolly Bugger. Another important observation is that the body appears small and streamlined while swimming. And finally, the crayfish is not a straight and level navigator. It swims and darts at severe angles and almost always tilted to one side, exposing at least part of its much lighter-colored underbelly. If a crayfish swims a considerable distance in a series of bursts, it often looks much like a leaf fluttering in the current.

What you will never see is a crayfish swimming rapidly with its claws extended out at angles to its sides. This claw angle only occurs when it has stopped swimming and is able to once again take a defensive posture. We believe this factor to be the greatest flaw in many crayfish patterns. Most of the pincer-out flies spin like a top when they swing through current under any tension. This negative effect is even more dramatic when the fly is stripped. The natural does bob and weave, and it tilts forward and back and to either side. But it does not spin. Too much time and effort has been put into designing flies to realistically imitate a crayfish that is resting or in a defensive attitude. The problem is that we do not, in fact cannot, effectively fish them sitting still.

Depending on specific river characteristics, the crayfish is probably either the number one or number two preferred prey of trophy trout. Similarly, leech and lamprey imitations are always important. When you design and make these flies, especially crayfish patterns, remember to think about *how* you will be fishing them. Will you be primarily dead-drifting? Will you be using the jerk-strip retrieve, a dredge, an across-and-down swing? Most probably you will employ more than one method and that is precisely why, in this group of flies, simpler is better.

Here are our favorite leech and crayfish patterns:

> 15. Woolly Bugger
> 16. Conehead Madonna
> 17. Galloup's Craw
> 18. Trick or Treat
> 19. Twin-Tail Madonna
> 20. Marabou Leech
> 21. War Bird
> 22. Strip Leech

We've said enough about the Woolly Bugger. As a final testament we'll just add that if you are in unfamiliar water, if you are in doubt, if experimentation has failed, just tie on a Bugger and stick with it. The

Madonna serves a dual purpose in that it is representative of both sculpins and, in the right colors, crayfish. Its seductive action and durability get high marks. Twin-Tail Madonna and the Trick or Treat are good examples of "suggestive" rather than "imitative" patterns designed for a specific purpose. Neither looks much like anything—particularly not a crayfish—when it's lying in a fly box all neat and dry. But when wet, both flies slim to the proper shape and proportion, have excellent lifelike properties and built-in action, and feature the proper colors to suggest a fleeing crayfish. Just about any color of Strip Leech or Marabou Leech will catch fish, but we have found black, olive, and brown to be most productive. Although tied similarly to the Zonker, a Strip or Marabou Leech works best with subtler blends of color, less flash. An interesting version uses dark brown mink for the wing over a blended-fur body of dirty tan and orangish brown. Not much to look at in your hand, but in the water it takes on the appearance and action of a night crawler tumbling in the flow. Enough said.

This pattern combines fur strip action and durability with distinctive colors, a sculpin head and profile, and large attention-grabbing eyes. It is being field tested now by its developer, Jac Ford.

## Attractors

In the general sense of the term, an *attractor* pattern is any streamer that doesn't imitate a specific food source. The word may make you think of traditional bright flies like the Mickey Finn and Royal Coachman streamer. In earlier days, streamers were commonly overdressed and flashy with bright colors. By today's standards they are outright gaudy, and almost all of them would be considered attractor patterns. Handsome older flies like the Parmachene Belle, Yellow Sally, and Jane Craig would be an extremely rare find in a streamer box today. Still, what is old-fashioned to us may just be spanking new and attractive to a trout. If a fish hasn't seen it before, it's new to him. How many trout in your home river have ever seen a General Practitioner? It's worth thinking about.

As the 1970s unfolded and precise hatch matching became the rage for dry-fly enthusiasts, so the trend in streamers became more prey specific. As a general observation, it seems that attractor patterns became much less popular as a new generation of tyers came of age. We were no longer happy with the old flies—the Mickey Finns, Gray Ghosts, and Royal Coachmen. We were on a mission to improve the old, but alas, much of the old did not need fixing.

There is a small stream on the Canadian coast of Lake Superior, near the very top of the lake. This friendly, tea-colored spate river fluctuates wildly with snowmelt and rain, and is relatively sterile. In the spring it hosts a run of supercharged steelhead, and in the fall it beckons salmon, lake trout, and the Great Spirit's most beautiful fish, the coaster brook trout in full-dress courting attire.

These September brook trout reach impressive size and are usually guileless and aggressive. They eat Woolly Buggers, practically *any* sculpin pattern, and (sometimes) nymphs. Once in a while, though, they will get uppity and ignore the best of the best fished with great care. Nary a flash at a Strip Leech, no heavy thud on a Zoo Cougar, no openmouthed charge at a Butt Monkey will be your reward. What to do? Well, what has always worked in the past is a return to a classic. Tie on a big Mickey Finn bucktail and watch those moody brookies turn on. This is fact, not fantasy. There is something about the yellow and red, the tinsel body, the slim profile that triggers a riot in this tannic river. Perhaps the brook trout, the trout of our grandfathers, is a creature of nostalgia in more ways than one.

The popularity of synthetics has actually brought a kind of renaissance to the attractor group of flies. New materials have sparked renewed interest in the classics and breathed new life into some of the old patterns. Add a touch of Flashabou here, a dash of Krystal Flash there, and voilà! A cosmic disco dace is born.

We find ourselves perched midway between the krystal-disco-epoxy craze and a commitment to only natural materials. We choose to abide by the requirements of shape and size, then add color and flash as attractor elements. This is nothing more than pragmatism. It's hard to improve on deer hair, marabou, and rabbit fur for creating the basic streamer, but Flashabou and Krystal Flash are superior to tinsel for adding streamer seduction.

A good example of a fly that could be justifiably listed in both the sculpin and attractor groups is the Woolly Sculpin. This pattern has a good, but not perfect, sculpin silhouette and an enticing, lively action when tied properly. It is not an exact imitation, but a fair representation of several creatures that might be on a trout's daily menu. We tie this fly in several variations, with an emphasis on natural colors when we want it to pick off trout hunting for sculpins or crayfish, and on bright bold colors such as fluorescent white, yellow, and chartreuse when we want it to serve as an attractor. We often add a few strands of flash material on both sides of the marabou tail to complete the effect. The color and the flash serve as the attractor elements, while the fly retains the general shape of favored food forms. This is a *very* good fly.

Why do sophisticated, pressured, large trout inhale attractors? Why would they grab a fluttering chartreuse Marabou Muddler, or a gaudy yellow-and-red Mickey Finn? We do not know and frankly doubt anyone does. What we do know is that big trout respond to one or more of the components of attractors at times when they're ignoring more natural flies. But attractors do not work all the time. When they are "on," they are usually red hot—for a period. But when trout show a preference for more natural patterns, attractors usually go stone cold.

Here are our favorite big-trout attractors:

23. Madonna (chartreuse, white, bright yellow)
24. Mickey Finn
25. Conehead Marabou (same colors as Madonna)
26. Stacked Blonde (chartreuse)
27. Woolly Sculpin (chartreuse)
28. Rattlesnake (white and yellow)
29. Grau's Tiger
30. Silver Fox

This list spotlights an issue of sorts. Generally, when we think of attractor-type streamers we think of classics like the Mickey Finn, perhaps the Royal Coachman. And even the mildly retentive reader will note that some of the flies on this list have also appeared elsewhere. In the past several years we've noticed that flies like the Royal Coachman have become less productive. And we acknowledge that this could be due primarily to the fact that we are fishing them less, tending to favor patterns that imitate the shape and size of sculpins or crayfish. As the attractor element, we simply use color and flash. For instance, Kelly's favorite go-to flies are the chartreuse Woolly Sculpin and the yellow Stacked Blonde; my first choice is a bright yellow conehead Marabou Muddler.

The Madonna, with its dual swimming tails, has a wild, erratic motion in the water. Like the Zoo Cougar, it flutters and swoons between strips and in the gentlest current. This fly does not imitate any one prey closely despite its Muddler-type head, but it does present a sufficiently representative image of several. The Mickey Finn just continues to work. Various adaptations include marabou and Clouser versions, and

Here is an underwater view of the Stacked Blonde. This is a big fly that seduces trophy trout on a regular basis. The best colors are yellow, chartreuse, and white.

they perform just as smartly. We don't know why and have stopped worrying about it—we just fish it happily. The conehead Marabou Muddler has such an insignificant sculpin head that it probably doesn't have any real impact on a fish's decision to strike. What does—we think—is its combination of wild marabou action and a bright cone at the nose. The Stacked Blonde is big and bright—easily seen even in murky water on dark days. It is an intruder that must be dealt with. Both the Woolly Sculpin and the Rattlesnake, in bright colors, combine lifelike action, familiar profile, and high visibility. Additionally, like the Woolly Bugger, they are so action packed and lively that it is difficult to fish them poorly.

Why any fish strikes, or why some flies produce more trout than do those with only subtle differences, will always be a mystery. We have, collectively, a huge pile of man-years of experience. (Never mind exactly how much; it's a bunch. we get twitchy when we start to think about it.) The more we fish, the more we realize that we do not *know* anything for sure, but (given our large and expanding experience banks) we are able to form some strong *suspicions* based on how large trout have re-acted over time. The only thing we know as an absolute truth is that everything we think we know starts with either the word *often* or the word *sometimes*.

Our measured opinion is that a big trout takes a streamer in re-sponse to one of two triggers—either territorial aggression (defense) or hunger. A pattern's built-in action, color, shape, and size all play a part in pulling the trigger. Combine such fly characteristics with the appro-priate retrieve and a synapse fires in the trout's brain. The strike impulse is turned on.

The best patterns, be they sculpin, crayfish, leech, or baitfish repli-cas, or pure attractors, evoke multiple responses—interest and excite-ment, anger and hunger. They incorporate movement, hue, and profile. All of the top producers have these attributes in common.

## Some Conclusions

Streamers produce results wherever trout are found. While the fish in every river, lake, and pond have unique characteristics, the larger preda-tors most often show a distinct preference for substantial meals. When you find large trout you find baitfish, sculpins, crayfish, leeches. Per-haps a given body of water features all of the major food forms, perhaps only one or two. Even if the dominant prey item is difficult for you to identify, remember that trophy-sized browns, rainbows, and brooks are naturally drawn to a hapless victim—a juvenile trout, a drowned mouse. Even high-altitude mountain lakes that hold very few members of the minnow, crayfish, or leech families will reward an angler who fishes streamers. And this seems especially true with leech patterns. Whether or not a trout in an alpine meadow lake has ever seen a leech, it's usually a pushover for a Woolly Bugger. No matter how naive or so-phisticated a trout population may be, they are all carnivores that live by their instincts. And instinct cannot be ignored.

When streamers produce their best results is, of course, variable. As in all fishing, the elements come into play. Rain, clouds, cold fronts, and sunny days all have an impact, but there are some peak- and low-activity periods that remain relatively constant. As we've noted earlier, the largest trout, the real trophies, are most active during the two hours before and after dawn and dusk. But the real beauty of streamer fishing is that you are not restricted to these periods. A well-fished streamer acts as a stimulant, a catalyst to action, even to trout not actively hunting for food.

It is best, of course, to fish when the odds are most heavily stacked in your favor, but that option is not always available—and even when it is, you will probably want to continue to fish beyond the peak windows. And it's good to know that you aren't wasting time. Varied techniques and a selection of imitative and attractor patterns allow you to fish throughout the day and still have a good chance of landing a trophy. Indeed, 80 percent of our own trophy fish come during non-peak periods, and we take a large number of these trout between 11 in the morning and 3 in the afternoon. These fish aren't hungry; they are responding to instinct with aggression.

Today's most effective patterns share one major feature with the great flies of the past: design. But much else has changed, including the world; otherwise we might never have been required to expand our fly selections. Unfortunately, the ratio of fish to fly-anglers has tilted heavily. In some (most) cases there are fewer fish per mile of water, and significantly more anglers in hot pursuit. Fish have become more difficult to seduce; more educated. Still, there are many who have trouble believing that a creature with a brain the size of a pea can become more sophisticated, and insist that a black-and-white bucktail is all they need for any trout that swims. We love to fish behind such anglers.

We face challenges today that anglers in the past did not dream of, but these challenges are not all negative. They foster new techniques, fresh designs, and problem-solving, analytical approaches that keep our sport ever young. Remember, it was not so long ago that folks said flatly that a steelhead would *not* take a dry fly, and that a bonefish would not eat *any* fly. Today's modern patterns are developed to meet such challenges head-on. They are engineered to meet specific needs.

# Fly-Tying Patterns

## KIWI MUDDLER

**Hook:** TMC 300, #2–8
**Thread:** 3/0 Monocord
**Tail:** Red Hackle Fibers
**Body:** Wool yarn, white or cream
**Rib:** Medium silver tinsel
**Wing:** Natural bunny strip
**Collar:** Natural deer hair
**Head:** Natural deer hair
**Comments:** Head is trimmed in the traditional Muddler fashion.

## WOOLLY SCULPIN

**Hook:** TMC 300, sizes 2–6
**Thread:** Danville Super Strong
**Tail:** Marabou, color to match body
**Body:** Medium chenille, color of choice
**Rib:** Palmered hackle, color to match body
**Collar:** Deer body hair, color to match body
**Head:** Deer body hair, color to match body—clipped
**Comments:** We tie this fly in every color imaginable, especially black, olive, white, tan, and chartreuse. You'll see a chartreuse

version pictured in the color plates. Trim the bottom of the head in the same fashion as the Cougar, and leave it fairly broad.

## ZOO COUGAR

**Hook:** TMC 300, size 2 or 4

**Thread:** Danville Super Strong, color to match head

**Tail:** Yellow marabou

**Body:** Pearl Sparkle Braid

**Wing:** Mallard flank feather dyed wood duck yellow

**Underwing:** White calf tail

**Collar:** Olive-yellow deer body hair

**Head:** Olive-yellow deer body hair, clipped

**Comments:** The Cougar is designed as a neutral density streamer. The flank feather placement is very important to make the fly swim properly. Make sure the feather is directly on the top. Trim the bottom of the head flat, preferably with a razor blade. The combination of the flat-bottomed head and the mallard flank makes the fly swim correctly.

Even though this fly was designed to be a floater, it also works very well with a wool head.

## BUTT MONKEY

**Hook:** TMC 300 or TMC 5236, size 2 or 4

**Thread:** 3/0

**Tail:** Yellow marabou plus six strands of gold Flashabou

**Body:** Gold sparkle chenille

**Rib:** Medium copper wire
**Wing:** Rust rabbit strip
**Throat:** Red wool
**Collar:** Pheasant rump
**Head:** Spun and clipped ram's wool, tan

## WHITLOCK'S SCULPIN

**Hook:** TMC 9395, size 2–6
**Thread:** 3/0 or Danville Super
   Strong
**Body:** Olive wool yarn
**Rib:** Medium gold or copper wire
**Wing:** Four olive grizzly hackles
**Underwing:** Red squirrel tail
**Throat:** Red wool yarn
**Fins:** Pheasant rump feathers
**Collar:** Olive deer hair
**Head:** Olive deer hair
**Eyes:** Optional
**Comments:** The grizzly hackle wings are tied flat over the body.

## RATTLESNAKE

**Hook:** Stinger—TMC 2457, size 10;
   body—TMC 105, size 6
**Thread:** Danville Super Strong
**Body:** Five ⅛-inch beads
**Wing:** Rabbit strip
**Collar:** Natural deer body hair
**Head:** Natural deer body hair
**Comments:** To tie the Rattlesnake,

first snell a piece of mono to the TMC 2457 hook. To do this, clamp the 2457 upside-down in the vise. Thread a 10-inch piece of 20-pound Maxima through the eye of the hook and tie a snell knot onto the shank. Next, slide the five beads down the thread to the eye of the 2457 hook. Remove the 2457 from the vise and clamp in the TMC 105. Lash down the mono, wrap it forward to the eye, thread it through the eye, and lash it down the bottom toward the bend. Clip the excess and glue the wraps. Tie in the rabbit strip so that its end is even with the point of the stinger hook. Add Flashabou, and finish with the collar and the head.

The Rattlesnake was developed by Ray Schmidt in 1998 and has quickly become one of our favorites. It is smaller than most of the flies we use but has produced well for big fish. The design of the body makes the wing almost foulproof; it seldom wraps around itself.

The fly is tied for the most part like a Madonna, although the collar and head are tied more like a traditional Muddler. We tie this fly in yellow, black, white, olive, and orange.

## ZONKER

**Hook:** TMC 300, sizes 2–6
**Thread:** 3/0, usually black
**Underbody:** Lead wire or Zonker
    tape
**Body:** Mylar tubing
**Wing:** Rabbit strip
**Throat:** Red hackle fibers
**Eyes:** Optional, usually painted

## MATUKA

**Hook:** TMC 300 or 5263, sizes 2–8
**Thread:** 3/0, black
**Body:** Chenille or wool yarn, light olive, tan, pale yellow, hite
**Rib:** Fine gold or copper wing
**Wing:** Four rooster hackles, natural badger, gold, or brown
**Throat:** Red yarn
**Collar:** Rooster hackle, color to match wing

## STACKED BLONDE

**Hook:** Keel hook, size 2
**Body:** This is actually the first wing—yellow, white, or chartreuse bucktail
**Second wing:** Bucktail, same color
**Third wing:** Bucktail, same color
**Fourth wing:** Marabou, color to match bucktail
**Note:** The hook is placed in the vise with the point down. This fly is designed to swim with hook-point-down, not up (as the hook was designed to do). We use this type of hook to build a wide profile, not to make the fly weedless.
**Comments:** The Stacked Blonde is a variation of the fly made famous by the late, great Joe Brooks. This is one of the best big trout flies we fish. We tie it in one of three colors: white, yellow, or chartreuse.

The first wing of bucktail is tied in at the halfway point of the shank and wrapped forward to the middle of the first bend. The second wing is then tied from that point and wrapped to the final bend, keeping the hair on the top of the flat portion. You will have to roll and split the hair around the hook to keep equal portions on both sides of it. Taper the hair and finish a little short of the eye. The third wing is placed on the bottom of the hook, on the flat portion near the eye. Taper this wing just short of the eye also. Now you should have a fairly substantial head—which is what you want. The fourth and final wing is marabou, placed on the top of the hook. Use two of the longest high-quality (strung) plumes you can find, and use the tips only so that the fly will have maximum swimming action.

If you like a little extra flash, you can also add a few strands of Flashabou at any of the wing steps. On some of the flies we also add a fifth step—a pair of dyed grizzly hackles down each side of the fly to give it stripes or parr marks. We also finish the head with a prismatic eye.

This fly is designed to have a big head and keep a broad profile in water. It worked well for Joe Brooks in its original form and has worked well for us in its modern form.

## ORIGINAL BLONDE

**Hook:** TMC 7999, sizes
  1–1/0
**Thread:** 3/0, color to match
  wing
**Tail:** Midwing serves as tail
**Body:** Silver Mylar
**Wing:** Bucktail—white, yellow, or chartreuse
**Midwing:** Bucktail—white, yellow, or chartreuse

## GRAY GHOST

**Hook:** TMC 300, sizes 4–8
**Thread:** Black 3/0 or 6/0
**Tag:** Fine silver Mylar tinsel
**Body:** Red or orange floss
**Rib:** Fine silver wire
**Wing:** Four gray saddle hackles
**Overwing:** Four strands of peacock herl
**Throat:** Golden pheasant crest fibers
**Cheeks:** Silver pheasant body feathers with jungle cock eyes as
   overlays

## DOC'S GLASS MINNOW
## (PINK BIG-EYED SHINER)

**Comments:** This fly is tied exactly
   the same as the Big-Eyed Shiner,
   except the third overwing substi-
   tutes pink Fish Fuzz for olive.

## BIG-EYED SHINER

**Hook:** TMC 8089 Nickel-plated
**Thread:** Monofilament
**Tail:** Polar bear Fish Fuzz
**Body:** Pearl Sparkle Braid
**First overwing:** White polar bear
   Fish Fuzz
**Second overwing:** Olive Fish Fuzz
**Third overwing:** Teal Fish Fuzz
**Fourth overwing:** Four strands of pearl Flashabou
**Underwing (belly):** cream silk (from a silk brick)
**Lateral line:** Pearl Flashabou
**Throat:** Red Fish Fuzz

**Eyes:** Prismatic

**Head:** Epoxy to secure eyes

**Comments:** This fly was originally designed as a saltwater sardine pattern, but we have found it to be an extremely effective big-trout producer. By changing the color of the overwings, you create any type or color of minnow you need for your home waters.

## TRI-COLOR BUCKTAIL

**Hook:** TMC 300 or Carrie Stevens, size 4

**Thread:** Black 3/0

**Body:** Mylar, usually gold or silver

**First wing:** Bucktail, color of choice

**Second wing:** Bucktail, contrasting color

**Third wing:** Bucktail, complementary color

**Comments:** The Tri-Color Bucktail can be tied in any color variation that suits the area you fish. The Mickey Finn (a general attractor) is a tri-color, as is the Black-Nosed Dace (designed to imitate the baitfish). Stack the wings one at a time, letting each wing extend slightly past the bend of the hook. This is a time-tested pattern.

## WOOLLY BUGGER

**Hook:** TMC 300, sizes 2–10

**Thread:** 3/0, color to match body

**Tail:** Marabou, color to match body; black maribou with olive body

**Body:** Medium chenille, color of choice

**Rib:** Fine copper wire (optional), saddle hackle palmered forward—color to match body

## MADONNA

**Hook:** TMC 300, sizes 2–8
**Thread:** Danville Super Strong
**Body:** Gold or silver Mylar tinsel
**Wing:** Rabbit strip, color of choice
**Underwing:** Three strands of pearl
Flashabou
**Collar:** Deer body hair, color to match wing
**Head:** Deer body hair, color to match wing—clipped
**Comments:** This fly is an absolute must-have pattern. For a size 6
or 8, we use a single rabbit strip. When we tie this in size 2 or 4,
we use two rabbit strips of equal lengths. When setting the rabbit
strips, be careful not to make them too long. If the strips go past
the bend in the hook they will tangle around the hook. Trim the
head in the same way as the Cougar—flat on the bottom.

The Madonna, like the Woolly Sculpin, is tied in every
color, but primarily yellow, white, olive, tan, and black seem
best. A two-winged or Twin-Tail Madonna in tan or olive is a
particularly good crayfish imitation. A conehead variation is
shown in the color plates. And it's not only brown trout that
inhale the Madonna: Kelly caught a magnificent Dean River,
British Columbia, steelhead on an olive Madonna in 1998.

## GALLOUP'S CRAW

**Hook:** TMC 300, size 4 or 6
**Thread:** Black, olive, or brown 3/0
**Tail:** At the eye of the hook—the tag
end of the palmered rabbit-strip
body
**Body:** Palmered rabbit-strip hackle,
rust or olive

**Pincers:** Two rabbit strips

**Head:** Spun deer hair, olive or rusty brown

**Comments:** This fly is tied in reverse order, with the head first—at the bend of the hook. First spin one small bunch of deer hair with the tips of the hair toward the back of the hook; a few of these tips will act as antennae. Then spin a second bunch for a total bunch length of about ⅜ inch. Trim the hair into a cone shape with the thick end toward the eye. This will keep the pincers slightly apart when the fly is swimming. Next, lay the pincers on each side of the hook with the leather sides on the inside or facing themselves. Secure the strips about halfway up the hook. This builds bulk so that the palmered rabbit-strip hackle has the proper shape when wet.

## TRICK OR TREAT

**Hook:** TMC 300, size 2 or 4

**Thread:** 3/0

**Tail:** Dyed brown, olive, and tan grizzly marabou (mixed); four strandsof gold Krystal Flash; two pumpkin-colored Sili Legs

**Body:** Medium chenille

**Rib:** Brown-dyed grizzly hackle

**Wing:** Orange-dyed grizzly marabou

**Collar:** Olive grizzly marabou on top; gold grizzly marabou on the bottom; two strands of gold Flashabou

**Head:** Black conehead

**Legs:** Pumpkin Sili Legs

**Comments:** Although this is a time-consuming pattern to tie, big trout really like it wherever crayfish are present.

## MARABOU LEECH

**Hook:** TMC 300, size 2 or 4
**Thread:** Black 3/0
**Tail:** Mixed black and yellow
    marabou
**Wing:** Alternating black and yellow
    marabou, tied in by the tips at the
    bend of the hook and palmered
    forward
**Comments:** This fly is a favorite of top guide Shawn McNeely of
    Headwaters Angling in Montana. It can be weighted heavily
    and fished effectively with the dredge technique.

## WAR BIRD

**Hook:** TMC 5263, sizes 4–8
**Thread:** Black 3/0
**Tail:** Black marabou
**Body:** Medium black chenille
**Rib:** Black strung hackle, tied in tip-
    first and palmered forward
**Legs:** Sili Legs, black with red flakes
**Antennae:** Two Sili Legs, black with red flakes
**Comments:** This fly was originally developed by Kelly Galloup as
    an offshoot of the Yuk Bug. Later our friend John Ricks Jr.
    began to fish it as a stonefly nymph. He found it to be unbeat-
    able. After John's success with the fly, we began fishing it again
    not only as a nymph but also as a slow- or dredge-drifted
    streamer. It was a very good producer.
    The only difference between tying this fly and tying a
    Woolly Bugger is in the legs and antennae. We tie in the

antennae first, then lay the legs on top of the hook in an **X** shape about a third of the way back from the eye. Then tie the fly as you would a Woolly Bugger.

## STRIP LEECH

**Hook:** TMC 300, sizes 2–6

**Thread:** 3/0, color to match body

**Tail:** Marabou to contrast with body

**Body:** Dubbing, color of choice

**Rib:** Copper wire

**Wing:** Rabbit strip, natural, brown, black, or olive

**Collar:** Hackle

**Comments:** This fly can be tied in any color imaginable. We like to stay with the darker, earth tones. The most common tie uses a natural bunny strip with a dark body. For contrast we often use a yellow or chartreuse marabou tail. The throat or collar is dark to match the body.

## MICKEY FINN

**Hook:** TMC 300, sizes 4–10

**Thread:** Black 3/0

**Body:** Medium flat Mylar tinsel, gold or silver

**Rib:** Fine oval tinsel, gold or silver

**Wing:** Yellow, then red, then yellow bucktail (top to bottom)

## CONEHEAD MARABOU

**Hook:** TMC 300, sizes 2–6
**Thread:** Danville Super Strong
**Tail:** Red hackle fibers
**Body:** Gold Mylar tinsel
**Wing:** Marabou, yellow, white,
  cream, chartreuse, olive, or black
**Throat:** Red hackle fibers
**Collar:** Natural deer body hair
**Head:** Natural deer body hair, with gold cone
**Comments:** All of the flies in the conehead series are tied in the
  same way as the traditional patterns. The only exception is that
  you place the cone on the hook before you begin. When we're
  using a cone with spun deer hair, we spin the collar first, then
  use two spins of hair for the head. The first is made with a
  normal-sized clump of hair; the second spin may need to be
  slightly smaller to fit between the first spin and the cone. The
  hair will spin easily and lock in against the cone. When trim-
  ming a conehead, we follow the cone's taper as a guide. Our
  favorite colors for the conehead Marabou Muddler are yellow,
  cream, white, and black.

## GRAU'S TIGER

**Hook:** TMC 5263 or TMC 300,
  size 2
**Thread:** Black 3/0
**Body:** Pearl Mylar tinsel
**First wing:** Orange and red bucktail,
  mixed
**Second wing:** Pearl Flashabou
**Third wing:** Yellow bucktail

**Fourth wing:** Pearl Flashabou

**Fifth wing:** Green bucktail

**Throat:** Red hackle fibers

**Flanks:** Yellow grizzly hackles

**Comments:** Walt's original Tiger was tied on a custom bent keel hook. His method of wing stacking was adapted for the Stacked Blonde.

## SILVER FOX

**Hook:** TMC 300, size 2 or 4

**Thread:** Black 3/0

**Tail:** Silver Fox Zonker strip over Flashabou accent

**Body:** Zonker strip from the tail, palmered tightly forward and clipped flat on the bottom

**Side wing:** Red Krystal Flash accents

**Throat:** Small red Zonker strip

**Collar:** Black rabbit hackle

**Head:** Olive and gray mixed ram's wool, trimmed to sculpin shape—wide and flat on the bottom

**Eyes:** Prismatic silver or yellow

**Comments:** This pattern was recently developed by Rock Wilson of Traverse City, Michigan. It has a truly wild, shimmering, slithering action and is worth the extra tying time.

# chapter six

# Equipment

Although it is not an absolute requirement, we believe that some specialized equipment greatly facilitates casting, retrieving, and fighting when you're dealing with larger-than-average trout. We'd like to present some basic equipment requirements, giving you a range of choices from known, reliable vendors without specifically recommending an exact rod, reel, or line. After all, it's your choice.

## Rods

It is an even-money bet that 90 percent or more of all streamer casts are made with a "general-purpose" rod, or one designed primarily either for dry-fly or nymph work. And a lot of nice trout are caught on these rods. In fact you can catch fish on streamers while using *any* fly rod (with any action, made of any material), from a 1-weight to a 12, but your efficiency and comfort will soar with a more practical tool. If you're dedicated to dry flies or nymphs and wets, and intend only a few casts with streamers to pass the time, it doesn't make sense to invest in a specialized rod. But if you have a serious notion to pursue trophy trout with this most effective method, then we highly recommend a specialized rod.

So what rod is the best all-around choice for the various techniques you'll apply to different situations and river conditions? You have already made the commitment to do more than just cut back a dry-fly leader to 2X, pick out any streamer from a small selection, cast across, and let your fly swing. It follows, then, that you will want a rod that will deliver a full-sinking line, a sinking-tip line, an express sinking-tip (or Teeny-style line), and, in rare cases, a floating line with ease and accuracy. You will want to be able to cast this rod all day, to execute rapid jerk-strip retrieves without fatigue, to drive heavy hooks home on the strike, and to subdue large fish quickly so that you can revive and release them safely.

Several "off-the-shelf" rods are ideally suited in both casting action and lifting (fighting) power for serious streamer fishing, but because model numbers, trademarked product names, and the actual composition of the blanks change rapidly in the highly competitive fly-rod market, we will suggest criteria for your personal evaluation rather than giving you a list of specific rod models that will quickly become dated.

Sage, Scott, Loomis, and Orvis have taken the time to closely study the requirements, engineer prototypes, and field-test fly-rods for the specific, highly demanding requirements of streamer fishing for large trout. This is not to suggest that other manufacturers haven't. Our guess is that you'll find suitable rods in your favorite manufacturer's set. Thomas & Thomas, Powell, Winston, Diamondback, St. Croix, and others produce quality rods. What's important is understanding the basic rod requirements and picking a model that meets them to your personal satisfaction.

The ideal streamer rod has a medium to medium-fast action, a powerful butt, and enough length to lift and steer sinking lines. The rod needs to be able to cast tight loops and load quickly for accurate casts of from 20 to 60-plus feet all day without fatiguing you. It must excel in windy conditions and have the muscle to set large hooks on heavy strikes, as well as the power and leverage to control and subdue large fish with dispatch.

The ideal rod length will vary based on personal preference and the size of the river you fish most often, but it is safe to say that the best *all-around* choice is 9 feet. The same considerations hold when you're selecting the rod's ideal line weight, but generally speaking the most versatile choice is a 6-weight. For example, Kelly's favorite rod is a 9-foot, three-piece, 6 weight. My most frequent choice is an 8½-foot, two-piece, 6 weight, but we both use 7- and 8-weight rods under certain conditions.

Handle and cast a few rods at a professional fly shop. Ask the staff or, even better, the guides who work out of that shop what they suggest and why. Cast the rods at distances from 20 to 60 feet with a *sinking* line and a *large* fly. Evaluate quickness, loop control, vibration, accuracy, and comfort to your own satisfaction. You should be able to feel lifting power through the midsection right into your hand. Remember that casting on grass is only a poor simulation of real, in-water conditions. It is like test-driving a burly four-wheel drive on smooth pavement. You won't know how good that vehicle really is until you hit the ruts and the mud.

# Reels

Unless you are an experienced big-fish angler, we don't recommend a click and pawl drag. When a big fish hits, you will have more than enough to worry about. Your reel's drag system (or lack of one), or palming the reel, should not be added to the list. Having expressed that strong opinion, we will underline it with the suggestion that it is better to buy a used reel with smooth disc drag than a shiny new click and pawl item. And there is a wide price range for good disc drag reels. Starting at around $100 and topping out near $500, reels from Bauer, Abel, Scientific Anglers, Tibor, Harris, Teton, Pate, Ross, Orvis, and others will give worry-free service over an extended period of aggressive use. You will want capacity for 100-yards-plus of backing in addition to the weight-forward line that balances your rod.

Some folks discount the need for a specialized rod and disc drag reel because they assume they will be fishing mostly for brown trout, and they *know* that brown trout usually present close-quarters, bottom-hugging fights; even big brown trout rarely get into the backing. Right? Don't count on it. If you do, you will soon enough be left torn and forlorn. You probably know how a large rainbow performs, and a fair percentage of browns and brook trout react similarily when hooked.

～

A recent client provided an interesting case study with predictable results. It was late May on the Au Sable River between McKinley and U.S. Forest Service bridge 4001. The plan—to fish sculpin and crayfish patterns along the rocky ledges and close to undercut banks. The client had driven up from Lexington, Kentucky, the previous day and told us that he had brought all the right gear based on a previous telephone conversation.

Doctor Sam had some previous fly-fishing experience—in fact, he had fished quite a bit in Wyoming and Montana in years past—but had just returned to the sport after a several-year hiatus. He admitted that he might be "just a tad rusty." His rod was a 9-foot 5-weight of first-generation graphite. It had a slow, soft action. His reel was a Hardy LRH spooled with an intermediate sinking-tip. This was a handsome setup and he had caught quite a few trout with it, but it was totally unsuited for casting large streamers and fishing them effectively. When Bob suggested he use another outfit, he declined; he wanted to fish his rod and reel, for a while at least. Nostalgia.

Sam started with a (relatively) small Trick or Treat pattern, a size 4, rubber-legged, marabou crayfish imitation. It was casting poorly on his soft rod with big, open loops and repeated forward-cast collapses. He admitted that the rig wasn't performing and agreed to switch after "one more cast." That, of course, was when the biggest fish of the trip decided to eat his fly.

A long, thick copper-colored blur thumped the fly within 15 feet of the boat and Sam struck hard—twice. The trout accelerated downstream—straight line, no hesitation. The little Hardy shrieked. Normally, the sound of a Hardy's drag is beautiful music, but not this time. The spool overran and the fish stopped, then moved right and back toward the boat. Sam stripped frantically to gather slack, but the trout was gone. The barbless hook had come loose.

The doctor sat quietly for about a minute. "Would you like some coffee?" Bob said.

"No, but I would like to use one of your outfits if you don't mind. That was the fish I came here to catch. Damn. How big?"

"Mid-20s."

So he switched and caught several nice fish, the biggest about 18 inches, but we saw nothing near the size of that first fish of the day. Sam called from Kentucky several days later with the news that he had just bought a new Sage rod, Bauer reel, backing, full-sinking line, and several spools of Maxima.

## Lines

For the jerk-strip retrieve the most effective line, by far, is a weight-forward, full-sinking line, usually a class V or VI. The full-sinking line keeps the fly moving at the same depth in the water column throughout the retrieve back to the wading angler or the boat. Now, we must add that this "same depth" is relative. All fly lines tend to make a streamer rise during the retrieve, but sinking-tips, even Teeny-type lines, produce a more dramatic variance than do full-sinking lines. This constancy of depth is important based on our observations, because it mimics baitfish behavior patterns when trying to escape. The depth at which your fly swims in the water column is easily controlled by your speed of retrieve and rod angle. Initial depth is controlled by the length of the pause—the wait time before the first strip—after the fly hits the water.

Many anglers are reticent when it comes to full-sinking lines due to a lack of understanding and, more importantly, experience. They think the lines will be difficult to cast and mend. The lines are in fact *extremely* easy to cast for distance (when necessary) with accuracy. They shoot well due to their fine diameters; they handle well, too, except for the difficulty in mending. But mending is not part of the program when you're fishing these lines anyway, so why worry?

The only drawbacks to these lines, in our opinion, are their tendency to knot and tangle when dropped in coils on the retrieve and the fragile nature of their coatings. You must take care to keep the retrieved coils *loose*. Watch them. When a tangle starts to tighten, loosen it immediately. Once a knot tightens it's virtually impossible to free without cutting the line. When you're fishing from a drift boat, take considerable care to avoid stepping on the line. These lines also crack and peel easily, and although this does not damage their sink rate, it roughens the surface, rasps your rod's guides, and significantly impacts casting ease and distance.

## Sinking-Tips

These lines definitely have their place. More anglers own them and are more comfortable with them than the full-sinking models. They *are* mendable and capable of swimming a fly at depth, and this is advantageous when you're using the dredge technique. And if worked properly, they can execute the jerk-strip technique with reasonable success.

When you're fishing deep pools, where fish typically lie at or near the bottom, a sinking-tip can be more effective (particularly if you use a slow swing or dredge in search of *hungry* trout) than any other choice. Sinking-tip lines in classes IV, V, and VI are much more productive with streamers than lines with slower sink rates.

## Express Tips

These lines are specialized adaptations of sinking-tips with elongated sinking sections (from 20 to 30 feet) and very rapid sink rates. The West Coast angler Jim Teeny is credited with popularizing these lines, which are extremely popular with steelhead anglers and guides who fish streamers under specific big-river conditions.

Scott Smith is a friend who guides fly-anglers to steelhead and trophy brook trout in the tributaries to Lake Superior near Thunder Bay, Ontario. He covers a wide variety of water types, from small creeks to the thundering, massive (12,000 cubic feet per second, with holes and pools to a depth of 30-plus feet) Nipigon River, the home of the world's largest brook trout and the last refuge of the magnificent coaster strain of migratory brookies.

Bob has fished extensively over several years with Scott and learned a great deal from this congenial, thoughtful guide. The most important lesson has been *not* to become too committed to one method or system. The rainbows and, particularly, the brook trout in Scott's home waters want the fly presented differently than do the trout in the Beaverkill, the Manistee, the Namekagon, the Madison, or the Yellowstone.

These fish, especially the magnificent bruisers of the Nipigon, want the streamer on a dead swing or a slow dart swing at considerable depth. The Nipigon is clear; its water has more visibility than the air in Los Angeles, and the biggest trout—rainbows, brookies, and lakers— hunker down and wait for a substantial meal. Our Canadian brothers fish differently up there. They have to in order to take large trout consistently.

Their specialized techniques often require express-tip lines. The line needs to deliver large, nonaerodynamic streamers in windy conditions and to sink them to considerable depth very quickly.

Scott feels that moderate- or slow-sinking lines are a waste of money on big water. Because a fly is pulled toward the surface by the retrieve of *any* sinking-tip line (which is an unnatural movement for a baitfish), he uses either a Scientific Anglers 13-foot steelhead sinking-tip (class V) or a Teeny 400 for really deep work.

Most often, express-tip lines are required to work streamers properly at depths of 8 to 10 feet and more. And these depths are common enough on rivers like the Nipigon, Yellowstone, Delaware, and Snake.

## Leaders

There is no need for a long leader. A large trout charging a streamer and intent on mayhem is not easily intimidated. It is focused on the streamer and its movement, not on the leader. Because the fly is *moving* rather than drifting, as in a dry-fly or nymph presentation, there is less time for situational analysis; the trout simply sees the fleeing baitfish, not all the immediate surroundings.

Most often a leader with a total length of 4 feet is ideal. If it's composed of stiff leader material, it will turn over a big fly with ease and drive through a heavy breeze without collapsing. Occasionally, a slightly longer (say, 5-foot) leader is desirable, but this is rare. Only under critically clear water conditions and a high sun in cloudless skies have we found it necessary.

The tippet section must be stout enough to continue the energy transfer from the cast (line) to the fly, and strong enough to absorb the shock of a multipound trout slamming the fly at high speed. Ten-pound test is our standard, with 8-pound test applied under very bright conditions, and rarely 6-pound test (but still *stiff* mono) if we're using streamers of size 6 or smaller under bright skies and in ultraclear water.

Kelly's favorite formula is a butt of 20-pound-test Chameleon Maxima 18 inches long, followed by a tippet of 10- or 12-pound-test ultragreen Maxima 24 inches long. When he feels a lighter tippet is needed, he uses a butt of 15-pound test 18 inches long, and 24 inches of either 10- or 8-pound test.

Bob uses 24 inches of 20-pound test, 10 inches of 15-pound test, and 14 to 16 inches of 10-pound test.

These are extremely simple and effective. There is no need to buy premade, packaged leaders. Just tie them up yourself with clear or ultragreen Maxima, Orvis Big Game, or other stiff, abrasion-resistant leader material.

～

Proper equipment is critical to effective streamer fishing for large trout. Your leader must turn over big flies and withstand the heaviest strikes you will find in fresh water. Your reel must be reliable and have a smooth, consistent drag. Your rod must be able to deliver accurate casts—rapid fire—of from 20 to 60 feet all day long without exhausting you. It should turn a medium-tight loop and carry smooth power throughout without jarring at the end of the cast. It needs enough leverage (length and power) to pick up line, leader, and fly; to quickly roll-cast without excessive effort; and to subdue big fish quickly. The rod does *not* have to protect tippets or deliver the fly gently to catch the trophy of your dreams.

# Suggested Reading

Bates Jr., Joseph D. *Streamer Fly Tying and Fishing.* Harrisburg, Penn.: Stackpole, 1995.

———. *Streamers and Bucktails: The Big Fish Flies.* New York: Alfred A. Knopf, 1979.

Hills, John Waller. *A History of Fly Fishing For Trout.* 1921. Reprint, Rockville Centre, N.Y.: Freshet Press, 1971.

Leiser, Eric. *The Book of Fly Patterns.* New York: Alfred A. Knopf, 1987.

Richards, Carl. *Prey.* New York: Lyons & Burford, 1995.

# Index